SURVIVAL FITTEST

A young Englishman's struggle as a prisoner of war in Java and Japan

ALAN CARTER

Published by
Paul T Carter

First published in Great Britain in 2013

ISBN 978-0-9575734-0-6

Copyright © Alan Carter 1986

The right of Alan Carter to be identified as the author of this work has been asserted in accordance with the Copyright, Designs and Patents Act 1988

All rights reserved. To reproduce any part of this publication, prior permission should be obtained from the publisher and current copyright holder Paul T Carter who can be contacted by email: paul@pcarter.net

A CIP catalogue record for this book is available from the British Library

Printed in Great Britain by Russell Press Ltd, Nottingham

INTRODUCTION

My father Alan Carter was held captive by the Japanese from March 1942 until September 1945. He was 19 years of age when he was taken prisoner. Many years later, when he took early retirement at the age of 63, he decided to write down his memories of the time he endured being a Prisoner of War. His memoir was completed in 1986, compiled from his recollection of those terrible times 40 years previously. The memories were still vivid but it is possible that some episodes may not be in strict chronological sequence.

Alan was the eldest child of Thomas Carter and Rose Allan, from Gateshead Co.Durham. Thomas had served in the Durham Light Infantry in the 1914-1918 War. Alan's grandfather Lawrence Allan (this was the original spelling of the surname but it later evolved into Allen) had enlisted in 1895 in the Durham Light Infantry but in 1897 he switched to the Coldstream Guards. He fought in the Boer Wars of 1899-1902, and was honoured for his efforts in the battles at Driefontein, Diamond Hill & Belfast. In France in December 1914, in fierce fighting at La Bassée (between Lille and Béthune), Lawrence suffered gunshot wounds to his head and arm. He was very lucky to have survived but had to be discharged from service on medical grounds. He died in 1917 as a result of these wounds and was buried in Gateshead with full military honours.

Alan was born at 35 Ellison Street, Gateshead on 23 July 1922, this being the home of his grandmother Ellen (Lawrence's widow) who had remarried in 1919, to Thomas Golphin – her house was just up the street from no.25 where Alan's parents Thomas and Rose lived. Alan had two sisters: Eileen Patricia (known as Patsy), born in 1924 and Rose Mary (known as Poppy), born in 1926. By this time, the family was living across town at 102 Sunderland Road. Gateshead was expanding in the 1920s and 1930s with new housing developments appearing high above the River Tyne at Gateshead Fell and, by the mid-1930s, the family was able to move to a newly-built council house at 22 Pilgrimsway, Sheriff Hill. During the war, Alan's father Tommy was in the Merchant Navy and his mother Rosie worked at the Vickers-Armstrong armaments factory. His young sisters joined the Women's Land Army.

Before the war, Alan had enjoyed a relatively carefree childhood and adolescence. He did well at school and enjoyed football, cycling, and playing the piano (he was very proud of a certificate he received for passing a London College of Music examination in 1934). In his teens he would often go to the cinema to watch the latest films and serials and in 1937 he decided he could not miss a serial, even to attend the wedding of his Uncle Lawrie! Alan was employed at Angus Errington paper merchants, as was his sister Patsy, when war broke out. He was called up in October 1940 and attended Recruit Centre 3RC at RAF Padgate near Warrington where he became Aircraftman 1125504 Carter (with rank of AC2). He then had to await a place on a wireless training course which took him to 10 SRC (Signals Recruit Centre) in Blackpool in December 1940.

He joined RAF 605 "County of Warwick" Squadron and there followed a succession of postings in Shropshire and Warwickshire: April 1941 to 5 SFTS (Service Flying Training School) at RAF Tern Hill near Market Drayton, July 1941 to RAF Baginton at Coventry (where he was promoted to AC1 rank) and finally, in September 1941, to the newly-constructed RAF Honiley near Kenilworth.

The squadron had switched from bomber aircraft to fighter planes at the outbreak of war and was flying the new Hawker Hurricane. The Hurricane had played a vitally important part in the Battle of Britain in 1940, operating from RAF Croydon. With a turn-around time (for re-arming and refuelling) as brief as 9 minutes, the Hurricane was able to spend more time in the air than the more glamorous Spitfire. After 605 Squadron's subsequent spell in Shropshire and Warwickshire, towards the end of 1941 a decision was taken to relocate the squadron to Malta for operations in the Mediterranean and North Africa.

In December 1941 Alan was one of the members of 605 Squadron who sailed in convoy from the Clyde. Some of them had been briefed that they were headed for action in North Africa, others had been told nothing. The bombing of the United States naval base at Pearl Harbour in Hawaii changed everything. Although Japanese aggression in China had resulted in an American embargo of raw materials such as oil (leading to Japan threatening American, British & Dutch territories), the attack on Pearl Harbour was still unexpected. The United States and Britain declared war on Japan and the convoy carrying Alan and his fellow aircraftmen was diverted to the Far East.

In this book he chronicles his experiences from December 1941 until his eventual return to Britain in November 1945. He was among around 4500 people taken prisoner by the Japanese in Java – after the fall of Singapore and Sumatra, the island of Java had been the final refuge for the RAF in the Far East and only a limited number of personnel were successfully evacuated prior to the island being completely overrun by Japanese forces. After several months of forced labour under the strict regime imposed by Japanese, around a quarter of the Prisoners of War were transported to Japan itself. Escape from the Japanese-occupied territories was virtually impossible due to the vast distances to the nearest safe country (and indeed the difficulty of hiding among Asiatic peoples who were visually very different) – apparently only 3 RAF men ever did escape.

According to a 1946 Government Report (HMSO CMND 6832), no fewer than 1714 of 5102 RAF men captured by the Japanese were killed or died in captivity. In other words 33% did not survive – very different from the experience of RAF captives in German hands where fewer than 2% died. Deaths in Japanese captivity were mainly from disease & malnutrition. It was a constant and sustained struggle to endure the deprivation and rigours of daily life as a prisoner of the Japanese. Clearly, those who did survive must have had great inner strengths. I have immense admiration for my father's fortitude in making it through 3½ long years as an unwilling "guest of the emperor". This is his story.

Paul Carter
Spring 2013

35 Ellison Street, Gateshead - where Alan was born in 1922 (pictured c.1950 prior to demolition)

Sunderland Road, Gateshead (pictured c.1960 prior to demolition)

22 Pilgrimsway, Gateshead
Photo: Terry Willis 2010

Alan at Pilgrimsway (c.1938)

Alan's maternal grandparents Lawrence Allan, who died in 1917 as a result of being wounded in action while serving with the Coldstream Guards in France in 1914 (pictured c.1901), and Ellen née Crawley (pictured around 1919). Ellen was supervisor at a munitions factory during the 1914-18 War. She subsequently remarried but sadly she was soon widowed for a second time. She died in 1963.

Alan's parents Rose Allan (pictured c.1921) and Thomas Carter (pictured c.1915) in his Durham Light Infantry uniform. Tommy was later in the Merchant Navy. He died in 1975. Rosie died in 1984.

605 Squadron badge featuring its motto "the squadron never sleeps" and the Warwickshire county emblem of bear and ragged staff

Alan in 1940-1941. During this relatively calm period before his RAF squadron was sent to the Far East, he was based at airfields at Tern Hill (Shropshire) and Baginton & Honiley (Warwickshire).

CHAPTER ONE

THE JOURNEY

On a cold, windswept afternoon on the 7th of December 1941 we, the men of 605 Squadron RAF, arrived at Gourock after a train journey from Warwickshire where the squadron had been based for the last few months (at Honiley airfield). We had no idea where we were going but were informed that we were about to board one of the large grey ships anchored in the bay, just visible through the mist.

Before boarding the small boats that were to be used to ferry us out to the ships, we formed up and the first twenty of us were detached as a baggage party. After spending the rest of the afternoon loading stores on to these boats, darkness fell. Therefore we had to spend the night ashore in Greenock at the army barracks. Of course that night we went out and had a good booze-up because we didn't know when we could expect to have another!

We were to find out that 7th December 1941 would go down in history as the fateful day that the Japanese attacked Pearl Harbour, bringing America into the war and, in a way, deciding our journey and ultimate destination. Perhaps we should have gone AWOL and saved ourselves all the hassle that was to follow.

The following morning we were taken out to the ship which turned out to be the Warwick Castle. This was a passenger ship in peacetime and belonged to the Union Castle company. Her normal route was South Africa and back. This ship was to be our home for the next 8 to 10 weeks. On board were two types of accommodation – cabins and mess halls. The cabins, depending on size, were shared by four or eight men. The mess halls, which had long fixed tables, were shared by as many as 100 men, sleeping on hammocks slung above the tables. These of course were cleared away when meals were distributed as everyone ate in the mess halls. When the baggage party arrived on board we found that cabins had been reserved for us, four to a cabin and, after storing our belongings, found that although these cabins were normally for two people, four of us were quite comfortable in them.

We sailed in a large convoy of about twenty ships, escorted by two warships. We headed around the north of Ireland and out into the Atlantic. The sea was very rough and of course the majority of us were sick, therefore we didn't eat for the first day or so – even though the food was excellent. After sailing north west towards Greenland and the Canadian coast, we turned south and eventually sailed into fine sunny weather. As we approached the coast of North Africa, we were met by schools of dolphins which raced alongside the bows of the ships and of course there were flying fish which skimmed along the top of the water, gathering speed and eventually becoming airborne. By the time we arrived at Freetown, our first port of call, we were quite suntanned. During the warm sunny days, we enjoyed using the canvas pool rigged up on deck, and also playing quoits and having inter-forces boxing matches and games. We had arms drill and lectures, carried out guard duties, and did look-outs on the bridge for submarines and armed surface raiders.

When we dropped anchor at Freetown the "bumboats" came flocking around the ships and the natives dived for coins thrown over the side, putting the money in their mouths as they surfaced. They also traded a variety of goods for cigarettes. For a tin of 50 "Craven A" they offered a pair of white silk pyjamas so I acquired three pairs of these for 150 cigarettes and promptly packed them away unworn to take home as presents. There was no shore leave as this area was classed a white man's grave.

Christmas was also spent at Freetown and I remember well the turkey dinner with all the trimmings together with Christmas Pudding, all eaten in temperatures that were in the high 90s. Little did we realise then that this was to be the last good Christmas feed for the next four years.

Having spent five days at Freetown, we sailed south after our Christmas festivities and, following an uneventful journey broken only by the "crossing of the line" ceremony when we crossed the equator, we arrived off the coast of South Africa. The convoy split up here, half going on to Durban and the balance including our ship proceeding into Cape Town, the backdrop of Table Mountain making a marvellous view. We spent five glorious days ashore with the South Africans making us welcome and picking up parties of us at the dock gate and taking us on sightseeing tours, also to their homes for meals. On one occasion four of us were taken by a family for dinner at their home. The first course was served on large leaves rather than plates and, when the leaves were collected at the end of the course, one of our party had eaten the leaf thinking it was part of the meal, this caused great hilarity for the rest of the evening. Unfortunately this stay was soon over and once again we were out on the high seas sailing east.

After what seemed to be an eternity sailing around in circles in the Indian Ocean (we knew by the position of the sun) eventually we received our orders and headed off in a south easterly direction. We were then informed that we were going to the Dutch East Indies, somewhere that few of us had heard of. When we got near to our destination the convoy again split up with the ships that had been to Durban leaving and sailing off to Singapore (which was under siege when they arrived and they were bombed constantly as they entered the harbour). Our part of the convoy sailed on and eventually arrived at Tandjong Priok, Java. We disembarked then moved into a barracks block in Batavia which had until then been occupied by Dutch troops.

RMS Warwick Castle, pictured at Cape Town

Troops disembarking from RMS Warwick Castle at the port of Tandjong Priok, Batavia, Java

CHAPTER TWO

JAVA & SUMATRA: February 1942

After settling in to our new accommodation we were taken out to the airfield which was approximately five miles out of Batavia and was the main airport for the region. The Dutch airline KLM operated from here before the war. We were still waiting for our planes to arrive, these were Hurricane fighters and whilst waiting we organised and dug slit trenches and air raid shelters (the Japanese had regular bombing raids in the area). We also unpacked the stores and spares we had brought with us. The Jap air raids consisted of about 10 to 20 bombers escorted by fighter planes, coming over the city and when in position, dropping all their bombs together. This was classed as "carpet bombing" – if you were outside the target area you were quite safe, but anywhere inside it was very dangerous as everything was flattened. The slit trenches were excellent for cover from anything but a direct hit, but unfortunately they became filled with floodwater so, if you jumped in without checking, you also got a cold plunge. Whilst on this subject, I remember one air raid when bombs seemed to be right on top of us. I made one dive to get into a slit trench and everyone else seemed to be jumping out – I could not understand this until something moved in the far corner and there, uncurling itself, was a snake. We had been given information on snakes during one of our lectures and had been shown photographs of all the deadly types – the snake in front of me was a type of viper (one of the most dangerous in the Dutch East Indies). I took one look at this viper and realised why everyone was jumping out as I had jumped in! In one second flat I decided that the Jap bombs presented a smaller threat to me than that snake, and was out of the trench and down the road in a flash. Needless to say, I tried to check trenches after that episode.

We had a Flight Sergeant in our group who had managed to acquire a motorcycle from somewhere and, during any air raid, he was never around. After giving us instructions that whenever the air raid alarm was sounded we should keep working until the planes were overhead, he would jump on his motorcycle and take off to find a safe vantage point to watch the "fireworks". When he came back he would give us an eyewitness account of the raid. He wasn't very popular. The Japs operated Zero fighter planes and, on one of the bombing raids, these escort planes were involved in a dogfight with our Hurricanes and Grumman Martlets. As one of the Zeros dived for cover, we saw something we thought was a "secret weapon" – as the plane dived, the wings folded back and it plunged into the ground with a terrific explosion, throwing earth and trees in all directions. Fortunately there were no casualties on our side.

Although the air raids continued both morning and afternoon, we did not have any raids after about 4.30pm so we could reckon on having a quiet evening. The city lights were still switched on and everything at night was normal, with clubs, cinemas and restaurants all flourishing. During the evenings we used to get out and "fill our boots" with food and drink without a care in the world. We tried all the Javanese, Malayan and Dutch restaurants, a different one every night and, of course, all the drinking clubs we could find. A typical night out would consist of a drink or two then off to a restaurant for a meal of 10 courses or more which would take half of the evening to get through! After that we would end up in a club drinking and watching any cabaret or singing acts that were appearing, before rolling back to the camp by midnight.

The local Javanese operated tricycle rickshaw taxis – these had a sort of armchair front that held 2 or 3 people, with the cycle rider behind. After a night out on the town, a group of us would hire about four of these taxis, sit the rider in the front and get on the cycle ourselves and race each other back to the camp.

One evening, not long after we had arrived in Batavia, a group of us were on one of the main streets when one of the cycle taxis passed us on the opposite side of the street and sitting in it was one of our friends, a Scotsman. We called out to him "Hey Mac" but, with the noise of the traffic, it was obvious that he had not heard us. So once again we shouted "Mac, Mac" but he went on his way oblivious to all our shouts. A policeman who had heard all the noise came across to us and promptly gave us a lecture about shouting rude words on the street. We couldn't understand what he was talking about until he told us that, in their language, shouting "mac-mac" meant that we were looking for sex! We explained that we were calling after a friend whose name was Mac – the policeman clearly didn't believe us and went away muttering under his breath. We could have ended up in jail.

By now the Japs had taken all of Malaya, right down to Singapore. We met some of the men who had managed to get away to Java and they told us some horrific tales of the wounded being bayoneted to death by the bow-legged little savages of the Imperial Japanese Army. The bombing raids increased in severity during the days that followed. We were then given orders to move out of camp to the docks where we found that we were to reinforce the troops on Sumatra, the largest island in the Dutch East Indies and the nearest to Malaya and Singapore, meaning that we were getting closer to our enemies.

We boarded an inter-island ferry which was packed with locals, livestock and stores. The journey to Sumatra was to take about 4 hours across the Java Sea and the Sunda Strait. The livestock was penned into makeshift corrals on the deck but, after we set off, one of the largest bullocks was forced out of the corral. With much shouting from natives armed with long poles, the unfortunate beast was driven to the side of the ship and secured with ropes to the rails of the ship. With ropes round its four legs, the animal was pulled down on to the deck. A further rope was put around its head and this was pulled back to expose its throat. A native stepped forward with a large knife (known as a parang) then started cutting the bullock's throat. Blood was sprayed in all directions and flowed into the guttering around the edge of the deck before disappearing through the scuttle holes and staining the sea red. Not the prettiest of sights and enough to turn any meat eater into a vegetarian. When the animal had at last given up the fight and all the blood had drained from it, the knives were brought out and it was skinned and cut into joints. Together with the offal it was carried away to the galley, then the deck was hosed down with sea water to clean away all traces of this barbaric ritual slaughter.

Later in the day, we were summoned for our meal and it was a rather tasty stew, even though the meat seemed a little tough. While eating our stew, we wondered how the natives would cook the meat from the animal we had seen killed – we were relieved that we would not have to partake of this. One of the cooks asked if we had enjoyed our meal and we said it was quite good considering it was from a tin. To him, this seemed to be a huge joke and he translated it for the natives. After their laughter died away, we found that our stew was in fact made from that unfortunate animal and not, as we had assumed, from a can.

Hawker Hurricane Mk1, RAF serial R4118, squadron code UP-W (pictured at Royal International Air Tattoo, RAF Fairford) Photo: Adrian Pingstone 2008

Page in children's alphabet book (from the war years)

Hawker Hurricane R4118 from RAF 605 Squadron commemorated in Battle of Britain 50p stamp issued by Ascension Island in 2010

We arrived in Palembang, Sumatra in the late evening and found that we had to march with full kit to our camp. There was no traffic on the dark jungle road and the night air was enlivened with light from fireflies which seemed to dance around our heads. The journey was about three or four miles and, not being used to covering this distance with full kit, we took around two hours to reach the barracks. There we were fed and promptly rolled into bed and slept like logs.

The following day, looking around and cleaning our new abode, we found that it was an army barracks which once again the Dutch had vacated. The Jap bombing continued and we spent a lot of our time in the slit trenches that were alongside each block. That evening we ventured into town and heard rumours that the Japs had already landed farther north on the island. We did not know whether this was true but realised they were certainly not far away with Sumatra being just a short hop across the Malacca Straits from Singapore. When we arrived back in camp after our evening out, we were informed that the next day we would be making for an airfield called P1 (Palembang 1) – this was in the jungle a few miles from Palembang and was a main defence for the area.

The next morning we paraded after breakfast and were told that, as we were to be a daily working party, all our belongings had to be left at the camp. We therefore turned out in our oldest clothes – I wore a khaki shirt, shorts, socks and boots and left behind my "best" clothes, uniform, shoes and, of course, all my personal belongings including camera, photos and all the presents I had accumulated and expected to take home. The transport arrived and off we went, leaving only a skeleton force in charge of the barracks. Our route took us through the centre of Palembang and out on jungle roads which were only the width of the trucks.

We arrived at P1 about 9.30am. As our aircraft had still not caught up with us, we dug slit trenches and helped out servicing the planes that were already based on the airfield. Around 11am we were having a break and eight of us collected behind a mud hut on the perimeter of the field, having a smoke and chatting about the state of things when the air raid siren sounded and almost immediately a large force of Jap bombers appeared overhead. They did one circuit of the airfield and we expected the usual carpet bombing but this time, from about 500 feet, they started to drop paratroops. This caused panic and confusion because we did not carry weapons to defend ourselves. Immediately after dropping the paratroops the planes circled again and proceeded to drop anti-personnel bombs through their own men parachuting down from the sky. These bombs were to catch a lot of us out in the open and caused considerable casualties. Of the eight of us who were behind the hut, only three survived as a bomb struck the road in front of the hut and shrapnel scythed through the straw and mud walls, killing the other five.

When we had recovered our senses, we realised that we were sitting ducks and would have to team up with the army who were the only troops with weapons. Right across the road, on the airfield, was an army unit using a Bofors gun to good advantage. We dashed across there and gave them a hand by joining in the ammo team passing up the shells which were in clips of five and quite heavy to handle. We stayed with this gun until mid afternoon and were bombed and strafed repeatedly during that time. We gave the bombers as good as they gave us until finally the order came to retreat to Palembang as the airfield was in danger of being cut off. We loaded the army truck with ammo cases and water cans, hooked the Bofors gun to the rear and headed off. There were five army and us three RAF men and we spread ourselves around the back of the open truck. I was sitting directly behind the driver on a 5-gallon water container, and there were another three men on the same side. The other four were on the opposite side of the truck, and an army officer was in the cab with the driver.

We started off down the road, making for the town. We had not seen or heard anything of the paratroops since they landed in the jungle surrounding the airfield but had covered only about one mile when we saw some of our troops in the ditches at the side of the road. They were shouting at us but we could not make out what they were saying as the noise of the truck blotted out their words. We had just passed them and the driver was stopping the truck to find out what all the commotion was about when, from the right-hand ditch, came a rattle of machine-gun fire. The driver and the officer in the cab were killed instantly and the truck shot forward, veering off the road into the opposite ditch where it tilted at an angle. Just then the guns opened up again and I felt the water container on which I was sitting getting red hot with the force of bullets passing through it. The shooting was all coming from the right-hand ditch so I dived over the side of the truck into the ditch where the truck had settled. There I lay quietly for a few seconds wondering what to do when I was flattened into the mud by someone jumping on my back. I thought the Japs had me and that this was the end. However it was one of the army lads who had also jumped off the truck. We lay in the muddy, smelly ditch for what seemed an eternity, with red ants crawling all over and biting lumps out of us, trying to decide what to do.

The Japs made up our mind for us. Two grenades blew up the truck and the Bofors gun and, as they must have seen us jumping into the ditch, they threw another two grenades which fortunately landed on the bank above us and, when they exploded, the blast blew over the top of us. I thanked God for the deep ditches that were used to drain away the storm water. We decided that we couldn't stay any longer and must scramble up the bank and get into the cover of the jungle which stretched right to the edge of the ditch. The army chap, whose name was John, went first and I heard the machine-guns and firearms spitting out their bullets and thought they had got him. But then he called to me "your turn, hurry" so I took a deep breath and moved up the bank into the welcome darkness and cover of the jungle. The Japs were shooting off their firearms whilst I was moving up the bank and into the trees. The whistle of the bullets sounded like angry bees and we could hear them cutting through the leaves and whacking into the trees. By what seemed like a miracle, we were unhurt even though the Japs had been no more than 15 feet from us. Why they had set their ambush on only one side of the road cannot be explained but it certainly saved our lives.

John was from Carlisle, not far away from my home on Tyneside. We continued to push on, deeper into the jungle to get as far away as possible from the road. As we penetrated the undergrowth and negotiated the streams and swampy ground we came upon an area where some of the Jap paratroops had been dropped. Hanging like festoons from the trees were the ropes and harnesses of the parachutes they had used. There were also bodies of Japs who had not survived the landing – they had broken necks and other injuries and some were still swinging like pendulums in the slight breeze that managed to penetrate the jungle. We also saw other bodies that had been cut in half by the shells fired from our Bofors gun, together with the other guns ranged around the airfield that we had just evacuated. The guns had laid a barrage just above tree height – we expected quite a number of casualties as the paratroops dropped through this "steel curtain". We were now witnessing these casualties and thinking that, here at least, were some Japs who would not cause us any more bother. After eating some wild berries we pushed on, leaving this graveyard and looked for shelter as it was getting quite dark.

We stumbled on and realised that we were on some sort of track as the undergrowth had been cleared away. We pressed on as fast as we could and eventually reached a small clearing by a stream. There were 5 or 6 huts alongside the stream, all raised up on stilts and with roofs made from attap (a type of palm leaf). We approached one of the huts very cautiously and noticed that the ground underneath was corralled off using brushwood piled high around the four poles which supported the hut – the hut itself was on a platform about 10 feet above the ground. In the enclosed corral were goats and two bullocks. The animals sensed our strange scent and immediately kicked up a hell of a din which caused the dogs on the platforms to bark incessantly. After creeping up so quietly in case the huts were occupied by Japs, what a noise we had started! An oil lamp was lit up above us and a head appeared from the hut. The owner of this head eventually became visible as he eased his way out of a space we decided must be the door of his hut. We could not understand what he was saying and no doubt he couldn't understand us either but, as he had with him a large dog and a fierce-looking jungle knife, we tried very hard to convince him that we were friends and did not wish to cause him any harm. After some minutes, which to us seemed like hours, he must have decided we were harmless. Two others had joined him on the platform and, looking around, we saw that the noise had awakened the occupants of the other huts and they too were out on their platforms with knives and spears to defend themselves. The man above us picked up a ladder made of two long bamboo poles and crosspieces tied with a type of vine creeper used as rope and dropped the end of this ladder through a hole in the platform. Gingerly he came down and the occupants of the other huts did likewise and we were surrounded by some of the most evil-looking people we had ever seen. They all carried jungle knives and looked as though they knew how to use them. In the flickering flames of the oil lamps, which were made from hollowed-out halves of coconut shells, they looked positively aggressive but we were to find out how wrong we were, and that first impressions are not to be trusted.

We told them our story in sign language, about paratroops dropping out of the sky (using handkerchiefs to signify the parachutes) and the explosions and shooting when we were ambushed, then our subsequent escape and journey through the jungle to their settlement. Afterwards we were quite worn out with all the charades we had had to perform to get them to understand. They held a heated discussion with much noise – if the Japs had been anywhere in the vicinity, they would have thought an entire regiment was about to attack them! They decided that we could stay the night – this they indicated by pointing to the moon (which was by now shining brightly) and moving their hands across the sky to show it disappearing. Grateful for this, we climbed the ladder to the platform where we were each given a sarong to use as a cover – we had to sleep outside, we were not allowed inside the hut because there were women in there and we were not permitted to see them.

That night passed with very little sleep as the mosquitoes came from everywhere and by morning we were a mass of lumps where we had been bitten. When the sun rose we looked out from our vantage point and saw that the small village, or "kampong" as they are called in Sumatra, was in a semi-circle around the bend of a stream that flowed just past the edge of the animal stockades. There was then a small clearing before the start of the jungle. Looking around from our platform, we could see that the jungle stretched out in all directions. When the owner of our abode emerged from the hut, we hoped that we would get something to eat as our last meal of wild fruit from the jungle had been a long time ago. We were offered a sort of porridge or gruel which, to our taste buds at least, was horrible – but it was filling. Then, as we saw hens around the huts, we thought a boiled egg would be good. But how do you use sign language to indicate a boiled egg? We pointed first to a hen and made a clucking sound. This did not go down very well and we realised that he thought we wanted his hens. So we tried again by squatting down and clucking, then showing the shape of an egg. We eventually made him understand what we wanted. He climbed down the ladder and reappeared from the enclosed corral with two eggs which he gave to us. Then, more charades as we tried to explain that we wanted to boil them – using a cigarette lighter and holding it under an egg. Still this didn't register so we picked up half of a coconut shell and put the eggs in it, then scooped some water from a barrel that was on the platform, and held the lighter under the shell whilst making bubbling noises. He finally worked out what we wanted and we could see his face lighten from a frown to a smile of comprehension. He lifted the door curtain and disappeared inside, reappearing with a small charcoal brazier and an old tin can which he filled with water and placed on the coals. We hard-boiled the eggs and they tasted delicious. We finished the meal with goats milk and a type of scone made with ground maize and water mixed to a paste and spread on a flat piece of metal placed over the charcoal. These also tasted very good.

Sumatran kampong (1940s postcard)

We stayed in the kampong for the next day and, eating with the villagers, we realised that their standard of living was very poor indeed. We helped them in a small way by collecting wood to make charcoal. On the second day, they put us in a bullock cart and covered us in straw in case we met any Jap patrols. They took us through the jungle, back to the road to Palembang. When they left us, we gave them all the cigarettes we had, plus the cigarette lighter and a pocket knife they had admired – small payment for their generosity. We felt very lonely on our own on that road, not knowing whether the Japs controlled it, or even whether they had taken Palembang towards which we were headed. We were missing our new-found friends and wondering what was in store for us. As we walked along we kept our eyes and ears open for any signs of enemy forces and for the sound of car or truck engines. We proceeded down the road for about half a mile when John suddenly stopped and said "Listen!" In the distance we heard the sound of engines and, as the sound increased, we realised it was coming from the direction of the airfield we had evacuated. Certain that it was the Japs, we jumped into the ditch to hide. Just at that moment the first lorry of a convoy swept around the corner and, standing up in the open cab was a dark-skinned officer who was dressed in a drab green uniform complete with steel helmet and who spotted us in the ditch. As the lorry drew level with us, it slowed then stopped. I looked at John and said "My God, they have caught us after all". Then the figure looming above us shouted "Come on if you want to get out – this is the last convoy going through to Palembang". They were Dutch Indonesians. We jumped up to road level and clambered up on to the truck.

Setting off for Palembang, we were told that the ambush on the road two days previously had been cleared away that day before dark. Since then the road had come under sporadic attacks, hence the need for convoys such as this. We arrived at the rail depot in Palembang in the afternoon to find considerable confusion as there were no trains moving. Gathered in the goods yard were the remnants of the army and air force. John and I said our goodbyes and joined our respective forces.

I wanted to return to the barracks in Palembang to get my belongings (and a much-needed change of clothes) but I was told that the barracks had been looted by natives and everything had been taken. So the bath and change of clothing I was so looking forward to would not be possible and I was stuck with the dirty, smelly shirt and shorts I had crawled through the jungle and slept in for the past three days. All my cigarettes, presents and belongings had gone but I was alive and that was the main thing!

After we had been given a meal of corned beef and hard biscuits which to me tasted marvellous but was disliked by some of the others, we were informed that the army engineers had managed to get an engine started. As there were open rail cars and cattle trucks in the depot, we piled on board and the engine was hooked up. With a cheer we moved off and travelled through the night, eventually reaching the port of

Oosthaven in the far south of the island. There we boarded a small ship which was grossly overcrowded – we were packed on the decks, in the holds and even on the bridge. Nobody cared as we were leaving Sumatra and the Jap invaders behind. As we steamed out of the harbour, rumours were rife – first that we were bound for India, then Australia. However we finally arrived once more in Java and, after disembarking at Tandjong Priok, we were sent back to the barracks in Batavia we originally started out from.

Batavia, Java (1940s postcard)

CHAPTER THREE

DELIVERED INTO CAPTIVITY

With our arrival back in Batavia, we took up where we had left off, working at the airfield during the day and doing the rounds of the nightclubs in the evening. I managed to replace some of the clothing lost in Palembang but had to forget my personal items. I had, in the course of the journey from Palembang, acquired a rifle and ammunition and I took the greatest care of it, cleaning the rifle daily and even sleeping with it, tucked up beside me in my mosquito net. After the fiasco of Sumatra and the ambush, I realised that, without a weapon of some description, you are completely defenceless and I had no intention of that happening to me again.

After a few days a request was made for volunteers who had weapons and side packs to "go on a mission up country". I thought it would make a change so volunteered along with others from our squadron. Next morning, lorries turned up at the barracks and we climbed aboard and set off, not knowing where we were going. It turned out to be a familiar journey – as we arrived at the docks at Tandjong Priok, there awaiting us was an Australian corvette, HMAS Ballarat.

HMAS Ballarat
Photo: Allan C Green

We piled aboard, about 50 of us equipped with a variety of guns – some had rifles, others had machine guns which had been rescued in our retreat. We sailed out of Tandjong Priok in the afternoon and once again rumour had it that we were off to Australia but, as the sun set, we were informed by a senior officer that our mission was to retrieve two new aero engines from the docks at Oosthaven in Sumatra and that, as no one knew whether the Japs were there, no risks were to be taken.

Volunteers on board HMAS Ballarat at Oosthaven, Sumatra
Photo: Australian War Memorial (306793)

As we sailed into Oosthaven the next morning, everyone was in a state of nervousness not knowing what to expect. There seemed to be no activity of any kind so we edged our way into the dockside. The two Merlin aero engines were in one of the warehouses. We managed to assemble a gang of natives to manhandle the crates in which they were packed. They were moved to the dockside and eventually on to the deck of the ship. In the meantime we had found that the warehouses were also stocked with spirits and cigarettes and, as Sumatra had now been abandoned, if we did not destroy these stocks the Japs would get everything. So crates of spirits were dumped, after the bottles had been broken. Cigarettes that could not be taken with us were set on fire in their warehouses. We all left with as many cigarettes and bottles as we could pack into our side packs so it had been a good mission as far as we were concerned.

Warehouses on fire after the mission to Oosthaven
Photo: Australian War Memorial (306795)

We arrived back in Java with the engines we had set out to retrieve so we had accomplished our mission successfully. We returned to the airfield to work but the Jap bombing continued during the days that followed and, with enemy attacks growing in intensity as they prepared to invade, eventually we withdrew to a tea plantation in the hills near Bandung to link up with the army, and possibly to form guerrilla units to harass the Japs. This camp was intended as a staging post on our way to the port we referred to as Tillijap (more correctly Tjilatjap or Chilachap) where we hoped we would be evacuated by sea to Australia. During the next week or so we lived off tinned rations and fresh fruit, plus anything we could buy from the locals. We also practised with the weapons we had available. On one occasion, together with two friends Joe Purser and Jack Roseveare, I went down to a village where we could purchase chickens. After much haggling we bought three hens to take back to cook for our evening meal. As we didn't fancy carrying live hens, the seller offered to kill them for us – we agreed and he promptly took out a parang and, holding the legs of one bird while he put his foot on its head, he stretched out the neck and began to cut its throat. His knife must have been very blunt as he continued to saw away but was making very little impression on it. Joe was from a farming area and said he would wring the necks of the other two hens. He picked up the first one and killed it with one twist of his wrist. By this time the seller had finished cutting the other chicken's throat – he took one look at the dead bird in Joe's hands and let out an unearthly screech. He jumped to his feet and, with the parang in his hand, dived at us. We grabbed the two dead chickens and took to our heels, with the seller chasing after us (we had to leave the third hen as it was still alive in its basket). We ran down the road and eventually shook off the seller and his knife. Having arrived back at camp, we were discussing the incident and trying to understand what had happened when a Dutch man explained that, in killing the chicken by breaking its neck, we had defiled the native's religion which stated that the bird must be killed by draining its blood. We had learned another lesson.

We heard that many ships in the harbour at Tjilatjap had been bombed by the Japs and sunk. Then, a few days later, we were informed that the Dutch Indonesians had signed a treaty with the Japanese and had broadcast that they would fight with the Japs against anyone who continued the struggle in Java. This put us in an awkward position as we had been relying on the Indonesians helping us and, if they were now going to fight against us, we could not carry on. Eventually we were told by our senior officers that we had capitulated and that we had to return to Bandung under white flags.

The next morning we collected all our weapons and buried them in a pit. Then, mounting the lorries which were all flying a large white flag made from bed sheets, we proceeded in convoy down the mountain road, back to the rail yard near Bandung. When we arrived there, we saw our captors for the first time. They were all short, carrying long rifles with fixed bayonets, and wore split-toe black sand shoes, knee-high puttees and a uniform that was dirty green in colour, topped with a peaked cap. The officers had better uniforms with polished brown leather boots and they each had a large sword in a leather scabbard. We lined up in three rows with our officers at the front. Our senior officer then called us to attention and moved forward to report to the Jap officers, one of whom started to yell in Japanese but of course not one of us could understand. After working himself into a frenzy with his shouting, he took off his sword and scabbard and hit our senior officer in the face with it. The men were ordered by the officers to stand firm as quite a few were ready to take on the Japs after seeing one of our officers treated in such a way. The Jap guards who had surrounded us, rifles at the ready, now started to push us towards cattle trucks which were lined up with their sliding doors open. They were shouting "koura, koura, hyaku" – we were to learn that this meant we had to hurry. With some kicking and cuffing, they moved us into the trucks. When we had been packed in our truck, two or three guards then joined us. After a journey that seemed like a lifetime, we arrived in Batavia and after disembarking, were lined up with much shouting and beating from our guards. We were then marched through the centre of town to a walled prison built by the Dutch – its long-term local prisoners had been set free to make space for us. The prison was called Boei Glodok.

Telephone No.: SPRINGWELL (GLOUCESTER) 2407
Telegraphic Address:
RECORDS TELEX, GLOUCESTER.
Any communications on the subject of this letter should be addressed to:
AIR OFFICER i/c RECORDS,
Address as opposite,
and the following number quoted:—
C7/1125504
Your Ref.:

RECORD OFFICE,
ROYAL AIR FORCE,
GLOUCESTER.

Date 15 APR 1942

Dear Sir,
    In confirmation of my telegram of the 8th April 1942, I regret to confirm that your son No.1125504 Aircraftman First Class Alan CARTER, Royal Air Force, has been reported missing and believed to be a prisoner of war approximately on the 25th March 1942 as the result of enemy action at Java.

    I will communicate with you again immediately I have further news and would be obliged if you, on your part, would write to me should you hear anything of your son from unofficial sources.

    Assuring you of the sympathy of the Royal Air Force in your anxiety,

I am,
  Dear Sir,
    Your obedient Servant.

for Air Commodore,
Air Officer i/c Records,
ROYAL AIR FORCE.

T. Carter Esq.,
22 Pilgrims Way,
Carr Hill,
Gateshead,
COUNTY DURHAM.

Boei Glodok Prison, Batavia, Java
(sketched by A Voordouw, Dutch prisoner of war, 1942)
Image Copyright © Museon, The Hague, Netherlands

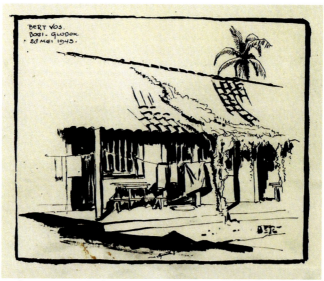

Veranda at Boei Glodok where many of the POWs chose to sleep
(sketched by Bert Vos, Dutch prisoner of war, 1943)
Image Copyright © Museon, The Hague, Netherlands

CHAPTER FOUR

BOEI GLODOK PRISON: March - October 1942

From the outside, the prison was a formidable structure with high stone walls that were black with age. When the large wooden double gates were opened, an archway was revealed and, as we marched through it, we came to another set of double doors which were opened to admit us. As we passed through these inner gates, immediately on our left, set into the walls was a large room – this we found out later was the Japanese guard room. There was a square courtyard with single storey buildings on two sides and a well in the centre. At the far end, surrounded by further buildings, was a smaller courtyard. The fronts of the buildings in both yards were set back under wooden canopies and were divided into cell blocks with iron bars across the entire face (and no glass at all). Each cell was about 20 feet square and had wooden trestle tables around the walls and down the centre. In the far corner there was a solid stone platform and in its centre was a hole – this was the toilet.

Into each cell the Japs herded 70 or 80 men and the doors were locked behind us. We sorted ourselves out as best we could, with some sleeping on top of the tables and some underneath. I was underneath the central table together with Joe, Jack and also Danny Meaghan. All our belongings were also under there with us, thank God we didn't have much. Our first meal of a bowl of rice each and a bucket of hot watery soup was cooked and served by the Javanese prisoners who had just vacated the cells we now occupied. After our meal we settled down for the first night in this new abode. Although we were all desperately tired, sleep for us was impossible as, when the single light bulb was turned off by the Japs at the main switch, we were at the mercy of mosquitoes that flew in through the open bars. Not only that, but the wooden tables harboured thousands of bugs that came out and bit us all over our bodies. Every time someone sleeping on the tables above us jumped after being bitten, we got a shower of bugs falling on us. When daylight dawned we were a mass of bumps and lumps.

Breakfast, another bowl of rice served with weak tea, was pushed through the bars of our cells. Then the Japs marshalled us out, one cell at a time, to draw water from the well to wash ourselves down. We were then locked in our cells for the rest of the day. Lunch was another small bowl of rice and weak tea and evening meal again rice with watery soup, all served in our cells. As we had to use the hole in the floor as a toilet, and as some of the men had dysentery, the stench in each cell was nauseating and this was only our first day. We were to endure a further three days of this routine before the doors were opened to allow us to circulate in the courtyards during the hours of daylight.

After a week in the prison we were permitted to organise ourselves – the first thing that happened was to get rid of the wooden tables, then we scoured out the cells, cleaned the toilet holes and rearranged sleeping accommodation by half of us using the wooden veranda. We then had to find toilets for approximately 1,200 officers and men who were now inmates. The only place we could find was the deep storm drains which ran through the compound and out under the walls. These were about 18 inches wide and 3 feet deep and, when a continuous flow of water was introduced by having taps at one end running constantly, the drains were kept clear. An area behind one of the walls was designated for the latrines – to use them you had to crouch astride the drain with one foot on either side. As there was always a line of men crouching along the length of the drain, the latrines were nicknamed "the boat race".

The officers were quartered in a building in the first courtyard which may have been the administrative building. The senior officer was a Group Captain Noble. The side of their quarters was directly facing the Nip guardroom. The cookhouse which we took over was further down the alley past the guardroom and officers' quarters. When our men had started to cook for us, we had to collect the buckets of rice and soup or tea ourselves. This meant having to pass the guardroom each time, there and back. As the Japs were an unpredictable lot, this was a nightmare journey. Outside the guardroom on a chair sat one of the duty guards and he had to be saluted every time you passed him. If a hat was worn, you had to stop, turn and face the guard, giving him a normal salute. If bareheaded, the procedure was to stop, turn and bow to him. This of course meant putting down the buckets you were carrying and, if the salute or bow was not good enough, not only did you get a good cuffing or kicking but the precious food could also be spilt and lost. We did this journey on a rota basis to minimise the possibility of the Japs taking a dislike to any one person.

During our second week at Boei Glodok the Japanese gave us forms to fill in, stating the type of work we had done both in the forces and as civilians. Our reaction to this was to put either the stupidest thing that came into our heads (brain surgeon, sausage bender, etc) or to state that we worked in a biscuit-packing factory, or anything that involved food – I said I had been in a sweet factory. When the forms had been in the Jap administration building for a couple of days we were told that some of us would be out the next day on a working party. So, after roll call the next morning, 50 of us were detailed for the work party – we took rice balls with us for our midday meal and were marched out of the prison. We made our way through the streets of Batavia with the locals standing and watching us. The Japs took delight in making us march to attention, with much shouting and pushing.

This first working party was to a yard where cars had been dumped and which we were supposed to repair. Among them were some nearly new American cars. I was with Joe, Jack, Danny and also Ginger Edwards. We decided to take parts off the new cars to "repair" the wrecks. The tools that we used mostly were hammers and screwdrivers. Needless to say, very few cars were repaired but quite a lot were wrecked! As we were marched back to prison after our work, Dutch women and girls cycling past would throw fruit to us then hurry away before the guards could catch them. We concealed these gifts as best we could and marched on. Sometimes the girls were spotted and beaten up by the guards but that did not stop them trying to pass food to us which was exceedingly brave of them. When we arrived back at the prison we were always searched but, by passing the contraband up and down the ranks, we usually succeeded in getting things through these searches.

After working on the cars for 10 days or so, we were told that this work was now finished, and that we would be going to the airfield just outside Batavia to repair the damaged runways. They must at last have realised what lousy mechanics we were! The airfield where we were destined was situated about 3 or 4 miles from Boei Glodok prison. On our first morning for work, we paraded at 8am and, after the usual fiasco of counting us (the Japs were never good at this), we set off to march to the airfield. On the way, we passed many restaurants and clubs where we had eaten, drank, and generally had a good time – how quickly the fortunes of life can change. When we arrived, the guards with their bead boards once again checked and re-checked our numbers then, once satisfied that we were all present, divided us up into groups of 25, with a guard in charge of each group. Joe, Jack, Danny and I were in one group and, after we had been issued with picks and shovels, we were instructed what we had to do. This was to dig out all the broken concrete from the damaged runways, mix new concrete and fill in all the holes, thus restoring the airfield to become operational once again. It was strictly against the Geneva Convention using POWs on war work but, as the Japs repeatedly informed us, they were not signatories to this treaty.

Each day the routine was the same – we worked until noon when we had lunch which consisted of a small rice ball and a cup of watery tea. At 12.30pm we resumed work and continued until 3.30pm when all the groups were reassembled, counted and marched back to Boei Glodok in order to arrive before sunset. The natives had stalls along the roadside and we would pick up the article we wanted and dump some cash on the stall. Sometimes you lost out by paying too much as you could hardly wait for change, other times we made on the deal. On one occasion I saw a stall selling tobacco, twisted in hanks like wool. I had one guilder and plonked this down and took what I thought was one hank of tobacco. Unfortunately the whole bunch was tied together and I ended up with a huge pile of tobacco. I jumped back into the ranks and carried on marching. The native seller was so taken aback he didn't pursue the matter – perhaps he had more than covered the cost from other transactions with the POWs. The men in my cell would be able to smoke well for some time but matches had run out. The only fire in the prison camp was in the cookhouse, which meant an excursion past the guardhouse. As the cookhouse was out of bounds except when collecting food and returning the empty containers there seemed no way round this. Fortunately some bright spark managed to use his spectacles to focus the sunlight to ignite a cigarette. We then suspended a rope outside the cell and, with one end slowly smouldering away, we could light our smokes from it. There was always a rope smouldering away whilst we were at Boei Glodok!

On another occasion we were again working on the airfield and, after we had been digging for some time, I decided to have a break. The only way this could be accomplished was to ask to go to the toilet (benjo) – I persuaded the guard that I couldn't wait and, when he gave permission, slipped off into the long grass at the edge of the airfield.

When I got there I found others who had also requested to go to the benjo and we discovered Javanese locals in the long grass, all with fruit and tobacco ready to sell to us. Successfully concluding a deal for a large bunch of bananas, I heard one of the guards yelling "koura, koura" at us. He too had been to the benjo and had seen us buying from the natives. We trooped out of the long grass while the Javanese sellers simply melted away. Ten of us had been caught and we expected a good hiding as we were not allowed to buy or accept anything from the civilian population. After giving us a lecture in Japanese, he searched every one of us and belted us across the face when he found the fruit and tobacco. When my turn came, he took the large bunch of bananas I had stuffed down the front of my shirt and cracked me across the face with them. I didn't imagine a bunch of bananas would hurt so much! After he had gone along the row, piling up more and more contraband, we could see that he was becoming very angry and we did not know what to expect. Saying "dami dami" (which meant we had done something very wrong), he made us turn around and walk away from him. Hearing the click of his rifle bolt as a bullet slid into the breach, we stopped in our tracks and turned to face him, having realised he had intended to shoot one of us in the back. I had decided that, if he did shoot, I would make a break for the edge of the airfield where the long grass would give good cover. Just then, an RAF Pilot Officer appeared on the scene and we explained that the Jap was going to shoot one of us and appealed to him to try and do something. He didn't want to get involved and walked away. We had more luck with a Pilot Officer from New Zealand – when he heard our story, he remonstrated with the guard, persuading him to allow us to return to our working party. The guard reluctantly agreed but he made a note of our POW numbers. After allowing the remainder of the work party to sit by declaring "yasume" (rest time), the ten of us who had been caught were made to work for the rest of the day, without any lunch break.

After marching back to the prison we were called in front of the guard commander. As we stood there in the guardroom, the Jap who had caught us gave his story to the officer who then proceeded to beat the living daylights out of us. In the meantime the New Zealand Pilot Officer had reported what had happened to Group Captain Noble who came to the guard house with our interpreter. After much discussion we were allowed back to our cells and were told to parade at our officers' quarters after "tenko" (roll call). We got a right rollicking from Group Captain Noble and were told that nothing could have stopped the Japs shooting us but for the fact that the next day was the birthday of Emperor Hirohito and that was the only reason we were still alive. However, as the Japs had to see that some sort of punishment was given to us, we were put on jankers and made to work in the cookhouse grinding rice for the sick, and washing and cleaning floors. In a way this was not punishment for we managed to eat a lot better whilst working in the cookhouse. Nevertheless it was quite some time before I ventured out on another working party and did any trading.

We continued to repair damage at the airfield, the Japs using a repaired part of it to work on their planes. One afternoon just before we left, we noticed the Japs running up the engines of a twin-engine plane, testing the maintenance work they had been doing. Next morning the guards were in a jumpy, nervous mood and kept tight control of the working party as we marched to the airfield. When we arrived, the usual requests for benjo were greeted with a cuff across the head and the order to "work, all men work, speedo". Later in the day we heard that a party of one officer and two sergeants had for some days been watching the Japs working on the plane and, when they saw the work finished, had decided to "go over the wall". They had done this the previous evening, boarding the plane and starting one engine. But they could not get the other engine started and had been caught and executed on the spot. We heard that the plane we had seen the previous afternoon had later been moved away and replaced with another which needed work on one of its engines – this explained why the escapees could not get one of the engines to start.

When we arrived back at the prison it was confirmed that there had indeed been an escape attempt and that all we had heard was true. The Jap commandant was furious and we had visits from the "kempeitai" (the Japanese military police) and a form was produced for every man to sign, stating that we would not attempt to escape. This was rejected and we were again locked in our cells with our rations of rice cut. The senior officer was also informed that ten men would be taken and put in solitary confinement without food or water until the forms were signed. After a week of increased beatings and harassment, Group Captain Noble issued an order to sign the form but added that, as this was signed under duress, it did not mean a thing. Conditions returned to normal and we were again out of the cells and back on working parties.

During our time as prisoners, our weight and general health was suffering and I was down from my normal weight of 11 stone to 9 stone. As we were getting very little in the way of greens and fresh fruit, the sick parades got longer every day. Most of us suffered from weeping scrotums which was a very painful condition, meaning that we couldn't wear shorts or trousers and had to walk around with either a towel or sarong around us. The medical officers did their best but had totally inadequate supplies – it was a case of using what they had on a trial basis. One day they would try blue unction so we would all be painted blue, then sent outside to lie on our backs and let the sun dry us off – not a pretty sight! What we really needed were the right vitamins to clear up this scourge. There was also an epidemic of body lice so we were shaved and had even our heads painted blue. Dysentery was a big problem and anyone getting this had the greatest difficulty getting rid of it. The jolly old boat race had more and more customers every day and the outlet under the wall would become blocked with the sheer amount of excrement flowing through it. When this happened we had long bamboo poles to push and help it on its way – this was not a task to be relished. Another problem was mosquitoes as they brought both malaria and dengue fever, which had to run their full course as quinine was not available. Unfortunately I caught dengue fever and, although not as serious as malaria, in the weak state I was in it was bad enough. The fever lasted 7 days and during that time I had to be force-fed with ground rice. When the fever left, I was very weak and found that I was now in the hospital isolation area, a block of cells taken over for this purpose. The cells were full of men with dysentery, malaria and dengue fever, some of them in a far worse state than I was. Eventually the time came to return to my own cell and I was glad to have the normal steamed rice once again, as the boiled ground rice that was served in the hospital tasted terrible.

Time passed slowly and the work at the airfield continued. In the prison a routine had been established – lectures and talks on various subjects were given to relieve the boredom, some of these being very interesting and informative as they gave an insight into the lives and pursuits of other people. During this time I spent my twentieth birthday and, while I was out on the working party, managed to buy a small bunch of bananas from a roadside stall. These I shared with my cellmates and the rice that night went down quite well, helped by having banana with it. It was certainly worth the risk of another beating.

Great excitement was caused one day as the Japs told us we could write a letter home. There was dead quiet that evening whilst everyone was sitting and concentrating on their letters. I managed about three pages on the very poor paper that had been issued but others who seemed to have true inspiration kept on writing – up to ten pages in some cases. Around this time one of the officers had made up a radio with parts smuggled into the prison from various sources and, as the Japs had regular searches, this had to be concealed at all times. After much deliberation it was decided that the cookhouse was the best place as it was out of bounds to all but the cooks. A false bottom was made in one of the rice buckets and the radio concealed within it. The BBC news bulletin was broadcast at the same time as our evening meal so the radio was brought past the Jap guardroom every evening by the orderly who was collecting the rice rations for the officers' mess. After listening to the news the radio was returned to the cookhouse in its bucket. The news was then circulated around the prison by word of mouth. Somehow the Japs realised we were getting news and intensified their searches but, although they turned up other contraband, did not find the radio as the cookhouse (in the Jap area of the prison) was never searched. About six weeks after we had written our letters we came back from our working parties one day and in the courtyard was a bonfire and all our letters were being burned. Thank God I had not put too much effort into mine.

We had concerts in the evenings and very good they were. There was a wealth of talent and this was put to good use. The off-duty Jap guards used to hang around the fringe and, although they could not understand the language, they enjoyed the visual side of these concerts, especially any slapstick.

CHAPTER FIVE

DEPARTURE FROM JAVA

As the year progressed we realised that the war in the Pacific was not going our way and that the Japs were still invading the islands between us and Australia. Consequently we were going to be in prison for some time. Rumours were flying around the prison that there was to be a big move and, when we were given a series of injections and inoculations, we knew that either we were going to a different prison camp or the Japs were using as guinea pigs to test their serums. Our questions were soon to be answered for, at the beginning of October, a small party of army personnel were despatched and the Japs then told us that some of us would be moving to a place where the weather would be different from Java, a place where we would see snow. When the "Groupy" (as we nicknamed the Group Captain) called for volunteers, most of us wanted to go as we had seen enough of Java and thought that a climate similar to our own would mean fewer problems with disease. However, in typical Jap fashion, they decided who had to go and who had to stay. Most of our group from 605 Squadron were chosen for the journey. That night there were many discussions as to where we were going and farewells were made to the many friends we had made. Addresses were exchanged and plans made for reunions after the war. After tenko and lights out, we settled down but not many of us had much sleep as our thoughts were on our destination and leaving behind so many of our friends.

Next morning we had the usual roll call and, after the guards had finally agreed the numbers, we had our breakfast of rice and weak tea then had to lay out our belongings to be searched before packing everything for the move. We were still in tropical kit and, as no other clothes were issued, we did not expect to move very far – at least not yet. In this we were partly correct for our first destination was another prison camp in Batavia called "the bicycle camp" – it was previously the barracks of a Dutch bicycle battalion. Here we met up with quite a number of old RAF friends, last seen in our early days of freedom in Batavia. Once again we sat around after tenko and discussed all that had happened since the good old days when we used to go out on the town and enjoy ourselves. The talk always centred around food – what we had eaten, how it tasted and what we were going to have for our first meal when free. The next morning, after tenko and a breakfast of rice, we paraded and found that some of the men from the bicycle camp were also to be with us on our move.

We boarded the army trucks sent to pick us up and, with two or three guards per vehicle, set off through the streets of Batavia and down to the port at Tandjong Priok. Our arrival here on the Warwick Castle earlier in the year seemed like a lifetime ago. The ship was called the Dai Nichi Maru and we were herded aboard like cattle and pushed down into the holds in the bow and stern of the ship. In the holds, wooden platform shelving two tiers high had been constructed on all four sides and we were crammed like sardines on to and underneath these platforms, together with all our possessions. The space between the tiers of the platforms was less than 3 feet in height which allowed us to sit upright but not stand. The platforms were quite deep so it was necessary to crawl over the top of anyone who was in front of you. As there were men suffering from dysentery it was not the most pleasant or hygienic place to live and sleep.

Dai Nichi Maru

This ship and others had previously been used as Jap troopships in their invasion of Java. In the centre of the hold were lorries and bren gun carriers being shipped out of Java but we had only the platform shelves around the edges of the hold. The hatch covers had by now been replaced, leaving the hold lit by only a few bulbs which were very dim. Our first meal on this ship (later to be dubbed a "hell ship") was rice and soup – the latter must have been made with potato peelings as they were still floating in the watery liquid. The rice and soup were lowered into the hold in wooden buckets on ropes. Trying to ration out this meal was a nightmare and some of us at the back of the platforms got nothing to eat or drink. However, by the time the next meal arrived, a system had been worked out to give everyone some of the food.

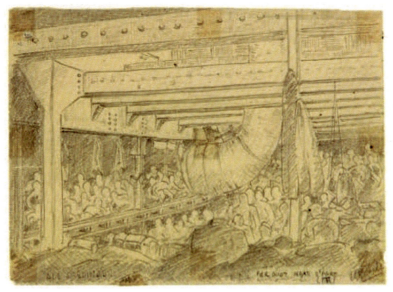

Hell Ship (sketched by W F Brinks, Dutch prisoner of war, 1942)
Image Copyright © Museon, The Hague, Netherlands

We sailed out of Tandjong Priok during the evening and, as I was against the side of the ship, I could hear the water gurgling past as we proceeded out of the harbour. There were no Japs with us in the holds. The air by now was quite foul and the sweaty smell, together with the rolling and pitching of the ship, made everyone seasick. As there was no place to vomit other than where we slept, it was disgusting with vomit and excreta all over us and the sleeping platforms. That first night at sea, there was very little sleep. Next morning the covers were removed from the holds and we were allowed on deck in small parties of 30 to 50 at a time. When my turn arrived – to climb up the ladder strapped to the side of the hold – I couldn't get up it fast enough to get some fresh air. When I arrived on deck, it was afternoon and the sun was so brilliant that I was completely blinded for the first few minutes. As I got used to the light I noticed that, over the side of the ship, there were small boxes balanced on two planks of wood – these were our toilets. To use them, you walked or crawled over along the plank and into the box. The floor had an oblong hole in it and, over this hole, you crouched and everything dropped straight into the water – OK when the ship was sailing in calm seas but a bit hairy in a heavy swell or bad weather. All of these benjos were in constant use as the men with dysentery needed to go anything up to 20 or 30 times a day. As soon as the weather changed and rain started, the covers were put back on the holds and it was back to the stinking sweat and other smells.

We continued in this way for three days. On the fourth day, after our rice breakfast, we were not allowed on deck as usual and we thought it must be because bad weather was coming. However the ship was not rolling any worse than usual so, if it was not bad weather, what could be wrong? This was answered by the ship swinging round and slowing down. Then we heard the engines reverse and suddenly there was a thump against the side of the ship which stopped as did the engines. The hatch covers were thrown open and the Jap guards appeared, shouting for us to gather all our gear and get up on deck. We grabbed our kit and climbed up the ladders. Some of the sick were too weak to carry their own kit so we shared the job of carrying it up for them. When we arrived on deck we found that the ship was tied up to a quay where there were many warehouses. As we moved off the ship with the guards shouting "speedo, speedo" and giving a slap or kick to anyone who was slow, we saw that there were working parties of British Army and RAF personnel on the dockside loading lorries with supplies from the warehouses. We had arrived at Singapore.

We paraded on the dockside and were counted by the Japs who needed to satisfy themselves that the numbers were correct, even though it was unclear how anyone could have escaped during the journey. We climbed on to the trucks that were waiting to take us to our new camp. We drove through the streets of Singapore and they seemed to be even more crowded than any place we had visited. Everything was apparently thriving and this did not boost our morale in any way as we expected it to be in the doldrums after it had fallen to the Japs. As we were leaving the city we passed a very large and forbidding prison – we thought that was going to be our destination but, as the trucks passed by, out of the barred windows, we saw white handkerchiefs being waved. Much to the annoyance of our guards, we waved and whistled back. We were later to find that civilian internees were jailed there, including women and children. This was the infamous Changi prison.

We soon arrived at our prison camp which was about half a mile from Changi prison. This was the Selarang Barracks, although everyone knew it as Changi POW camp. It was a whole village of army barracks and houses, completely surrounded by a double fence of barbed wire. At the gates we dismounted and the Jap guards marshalled us into the camp. We later found out that the Japs stayed outside the camp and that it was run and administered by British officers with Indian guards. The camp was well organised, even though the food was no different nor more plentiful than we had grown used to. We were placed in an empty barracks block and were allowed to wander around at will within the perimeter of the barbed wire. After Boei Glodok it almost felt like we were free again. As well as the space to walk around, the sleeping accommodation was certainly better as we had twice the room we had in Java. And it was sheer luxury compared with the hell ship.

We wandered among the different rows of barracks, all named after famous regiments, and met soldiers and airmen who had been captured in Singapore when it fell. Some of them had never been out of the camp since they arrived and their only experience of the Japs had been in the initial surrender. They were interested in our stories from Sumatra and Java and there were many group discussions. Others that we met had been out on working parties and most of them were still working on various sites both in the city and on the docks. They had some fantastic stories to tell of the first few working parties when the Japs hadn't yet sorted themselves out and each working party had only one or two guards. They had been allowed quite a lot of leeway. One group of POWs had been sent to repair part of a road on the dockside and were given the usual picks and shovels. They were approached by some Chinese who wanted to buy black-market petrol. As this was a good opportunity to get some extra food, they asked the guard whether they could have a petrol-driven rolling machine and he said that it would be OK if they could find one for themselves. The outcome was that every day a ration of petrol was drawn in cans for a non-existent roller! This was promptly given to the Chinese in exchange for food and medicine for the sick. This went on for weeks until the road repair job was completed – the guards were so lax that they never discovered that the roller did not exist. Such working parties were used to collect a variety of things that were needed in the camp. As time went by, the Japs became more organised and started using Koreans and Indians as guards – life on the working parties was then not so good.

Selarang Barracks, Changi, Singapore
Photo: RAASC 90 Tpt. Pl. (via Bill Desmet, 2/30 Battalion AIF)

For us in the "Java contingent" life was carrying on smoothly except for the usual small rations of rice. Our stomachs seemed to have shrunk to accept these small amounts and, as we were not having to work, we could put up with this. The concert parties were again hard at work – some of the shows were most professional and would not have been out of place on the stage back home. How they conjured up the costumes I do not know but some of them were quite outstanding. However our stay in Changi was coming to an end.

After being in a limbo-like existence for about two weeks, we were told to pack our kit as we would be moving out next morning. As in Boei Glodok, we went around the many new friends we had acquired and said our farewells as we did not expect to meet again. The next morning we had our roll call, the usual breakfast of rice with a cup of watery tea and, after collecting our belongings, marched off to the guardroom at the entrance to the camp. There, waiting for us, were Jap and Korean guards, and a number of trucks. We had two guards in the back with us, plus one in the cab with the driver. We set off and travelled past the towering block of Changi prison, with the pathetic little handkerchiefs still being waved from the tiny windows of the cells, back to Singapore docks. Once again a rusty old steamer was awaiting us, this was the Tofuku Maru. We lined up on the dockside with the usual kicking and cuffing from the guards and, after being counted three or four times, we embarked on our floating prison.

CHAPTER SIX

THE TOFUKU MARU

When we boarded the Tofuku Maru we realised that this ship had the same layout as the one that had brought us from Java to Singapore – with holds fore and aft, each fitted with the same type of sleeping platforms on all four sides. This time, I was in the last batch to go into the foreward hold and, as all the space on the platforms had been taken up, I had to live and sleep nearer to the centre, just under the hatch. This was a great improvement on my last journey when I had been right at the back where the air was pretty foul. Dumped in the centre of the hold was a consignment of loose iron ore on top of which there were various vehicles: lorries, bren gun carriers and cars, none of them properly fastened down. As we settled down I realised that Joe and Jack were on the platforms but that others in our group must be in the hold at the stern of the ship. My companions on either side of me were called Jimmy and Peter. There were no guards with us in the hold which meant we could organise the rationing of food, water and anything else that cropped up. However on deck it was a different matter with guards prowling around constantly. Our food consisted of two meals a day made up of boiled rice and very watery soup with either daikon (a kind of radish) or potato peelings floating on top – it tasted like dishwater without the grease. Meals were lowered down to us in wooden barrels. If the barrel caught the side of the hatch and the food spilled on to the iron ore, it was a case of either scraping it up, and getting some iron into our diet, or doing without. Each man's ration was a loosely-packed cup of rice and a cup of the soup – these were wolfed down in minutes and did not satisfy our hunger.

We heard the crew preparing to cast off then, with a rumble from the engines, we left the dockside. After our evening meal we spent some time debating our likely destination and engaging in our usual topics of conversation: food, what was happening at home and whether our families knew that we were still alive – especially after the fiasco of the letters we wrote in Java. That first night was spent with very little sleep – with the hatch covers closed, there was very little air. Toilet facilities in the hold were again virtually non-existent, just two or three wooden barrels placed on the iron ore. These were quickly filled and overflowed as there was nowhere to empty them. Once again we had to get accustomed to the overpowering stench that seemed to be always present.

Tofuku Maru

Next morning, after the first of our two daily meals, the hatch covers were removed and the sun shining down into the hold revived our spirits. The air coming in was warm and fresh, with the salty tang of the sea. After a long discussion, the Japs decided that we could go up on deck as long as we stayed close to the hold. This was a great relief as all of us now had the use of the wooden toilet boxes that were suspended over the sides of the ship. We also had our first funeral ceremony as we buried at sea a POW who had died from amoebic dysentery. There must have been hundreds of us in each hold, therefore the decks were very crowded. The guards prowled around all the time and we were also under constant surveillance from the bridge. Joe, Jack and I found ourselves a corner and shared a cigarette we had scrounged from one of the guards by showing him some photos we had with us – mothers, fathers, wives, girlfriends, children. The Japs were always interested in seeing photos of British people. We stayed on deck right through the day and our evening meal was also served on deck – much better than down in the hold. After the meal we were marshalled down into the holds for our second night on board. Our sleep was better, even though the hatch covers had been replaced. This pattern continued for the next day and, whilst on deck, we could see land in the distance. Some of our companions told us that this was the coast of Malaya – they had been stationed there before the war. After the second day we noticed that we were now sailing in open seas, with no sight of land.

Hell Ship: 450 POWs in one hold (sketched by Henri de Fremery, Dutch prisoner of war)
Image Copyright © Museon, The Hague, Netherlands

After discussions between our officers and the Japs, when it was conceded that we could hardly escape whilst at sea, we were allowed to stay on deck every day. The sick, instead of having to climb up and down the ladders every day, were allowed to stay on deck day and night, in a sick bay made of canvas tarpaulins. Another concession was that, until we hit bad weather, the hatch covers could stay open to ventilate the holds and give us at least some fresh air. We also managed to have hoses rigged up on deck in case of fire and, when these were being tested, we contrived to have them turned on us, thus giving us a much-needed bath. We had not washed or bathed since leaving Changi and, with the iron ore combining with the sweat of our bodies, we looked more like Red Indians than white POWs!

After about four days at sea, we were all very excited when land was again spotted and this time we seemed to be sailing towards it – was this to be our new home? As we drew nearer, everyone (including the sick) was herded back down below and the hatch covers were partly replaced. Our evening meal arrived earlier than usual and, as we settled down, we wondered where this place could be. As darkness fell we came alongside with a bump and the engines stopped. We waited for the guards to come and order us on deck to move off the ship but nothing happened. We could see from the small patch of sky being illuminated that the docks were ablaze with lights. Therefore, wherever we were, the population were not afraid of air raids. This did not do much for our morale as we had now been prisoners for about eight months and were slowly starving. We had thought we may be attacked by submarines but thank God this had not happened. While the crew were busy on deck we heard someone speaking French and, when one of our men climbed to the top of the ladder to take a look, he could see white people working on the dockside and on the deck of our ship, loading foodstuffs aboard. We were berthed at the side of a wide river. We eventually found out that this was Saigon and that the people here in French Indochina (modern day Vietnam) were not captives.

Next day, after completing the loading, we moved down the river and, as we had been kept down in the holds during our stay in port, we were glad to be on our way once again as we were allowed up on deck – at least after we had cleared the mouth of the river. When we climbed out of the holds and into the sunlight, we had to rig up our sickbays then get the sick men out of the holds – not an easy task. We found that, during the night, another death had occurred (once again through dysentery) so the body was wrapped in canvas and, with a prayer, slid over the side of the ship. This time the Japs did not attend the burial nor did we have the ceremony that they had provided for the occasion of the first burial at sea. For a few days after leaving Saigon we had pieces of pumpkin and greens in our soup – in one way this was good as it kept beri-beri at bay but, to the men with dysentery and queasy stomachs, it was disastrous as the greens made their visits to the benjo almost constant. We had another two burial services during that week as our sick gave up hope and died.

Joe, Jack and I had found ourselves jobs working in the stokehole, shovelling coal out of the bunkers for the Japs to stoke up the fires to keep the ship's steam up. We worked three 8-hour shifts, changing over with other POWs who were also working down the coal hole. The work was arduous with little rest but the benefit was that we got Jap-style rations whilst working. These consisted of good portions of white rice, together with either soup or a little dried fish. We also had a hot shower after finishing work and cigarettes were given to us by the Jap stokers. There was only one big drawback – if the ship was attacked then we were certainly doomed for we were in the lowest part of the ship. The rest of the lads were having a rough time with very short rations and many were going down with dysentery. We shared our extra food with some of our friends but this helped only a few.

Hell Ship: queuing for the benjo (sketched by unknown artist)
Image Copyright © Museon, The Hague, Netherlands

During this voyage I found that, whilst some men were dying and others were perpetually running to the toilets, I seemed to go only once a week or less. This was to catch up with me later. The weather had by now grown a lot colder and, with us still being dressed in tropical shorts and shirts, we were glad to get back down the hold each evening. It was a lot warmer there than on deck. As the seas were quite rough, the hatch covers had been replaced and were kept closed. This stopped the heat from escaping. Bad weather was a curse to us as we were not allowed as long on deck during the day and, trying to crawl along the planks to the benjo box was hazardous as the ship rolled. The Jap stokers told us that such bad weather was good as it kept American submarines away. This was the first news that our ships were operating in these waters. We were also informed that one convoy had been badly mauled by submarines and many men lost – this really cheered us up! As the ships transporting POWs were not marked, and were also carrying war materials, we now realised how much we were at risk. To the Americans, we were an enemy cargo-carrying vessel.

After a week at sea we again saw land and, as we approached, it seemed quite mountainous. When we had been working the previous day, the Japs had said that our next port of call was Takao on the island of Formosa (Taiwan) but that we would not be disembarking there – our destination was to be Japan. We anchored in the bay and took on fresh supplies from barges which came alongside. The workmen were quite friendly and said that some of our POWs had been put to work in the Taiwanese salt mines. We didn't fancy that. This was to be our only contact for, during the night, we sailed – making north towards Japan. Next day, as I was working in the stokehole, the Japs were excited and highly delighted that they were on their way home. They even became generous with their cigarettes and food, and an apple for each of us who had been working with them. In the showers, which we shared with the Jap stokers after work, they said they had been away from Japan since the invasion of Malaya and that the ship had carried some of the troops who had been landed for the invasion.

During the next week of our voyage north, the weather became a lot colder with flurries of snow mixed in with the rain. Most of the Dutch Indonesian POWs had never seen snow, nor had they contended with icy winds such as the cold wind which was now blowing. The Jap crew and guards grew more excited as the days passed and the distance to their homeland shortened. We prisoners too would be glad to vacate the ship as our death toll had grown considerably since leaving Singapore and every day brought further deaths from dysentery. Joe, Jack and I were still working in the stokehole. I think that, in a way, this work was our salvation because it occupied our minds and bodies as well as providing us with a means of obtaining extra food – a life saver in the conditions we were living in. Around 30 of our men had died during the four weeks we had been on the Tofuku Maru.

As we drew nearer to Japan we were beginning to pass small boats trawling for fish. They appeared to work in groups with a large mother/factory ship guarding them and collecting the catches. The temporary sick bays and shelters on the deck of our ship were dismantled and all POWs except those working were again moved back to their billets in the holds. The Jap stokers informed us that the next day would be our final working day as we would reach port that night. Our feelings were mixed – we did not know whether to feel relieved that were at last arriving at our destination, or sorry to be leaving the work that, in a strange way, we had quite enjoyed.

Next day, we started work early and as usual it was all go, shovelling coal into barrows and moving it to the hatches where we dumped it for the stokers on the other side of the bulkhead – they fed it into the fires to generate steam to drive the ship. When we stopped for lunch, which we had in relays as usual, the stokers had provided rice, fish and an apple for each us, together with a pot of green tea, and finished off with a satisfying cigarette – to us this was a banquet! We were then back at work, allowing the men on the second shift to have their food. When our work was finished we had our last shower and were each given a packet of 10 cigarettes. When we turned in for the night, the ship was still at sea with no visible signs of land. However, when we woke the next morning and collected our tubs of rice, there were mountainous peaks discernible in the distance. After our meal we gathered together our few belongings and packed them in readiness for leaving the ship. When we made port, there was nothing to do but sit waiting for the guards to call us up on deck.

It was midday when we finally arrived and tied up at the dockside. The guards informed us that this was Moji, a port in southern Japan. With the usual shouts of "koura, speedo" we were bundled up on deck where we were formed up into three lines and counted. We were then formed into a single line which snaked around the deck. There was a group of Japanese civilians on the bridge of the ship and, as I was some distance from the head of the line, I had a good view of what was happening. Those at the beginning of the line were climbing the ladder on one side of the bridge, then going back down the ladder on the other side. They were then disembarking to form up on the quayside. When my turn came, and I climbed up and stepped on to the bridge, there in front of me was a woman in a white coat who I took to be a doctor. She was accompanied by medical orderlies and, on the table beside her, there was a pile of glass rods. An interpreter asked for my name and rank then, after noting this on a clipboard, told me to drop my trousers and bend over. The doctor took a glass rod and stuck it up my behind. This must have been their way of testing our stools for dysentery etc. It certainly wasn't a pleasant experience for us. The civilians on the dockside, including some women, seemed to enjoy the spectacle. After everyone had been examined we were marched away. We boarded a train – not with the customary cattle wagons but with real carriages. As we climbed aboard we were each given a wooden box about 8" x 5" x 3" and, when we settled in our seats, we found that these boxes contained boiled rice with two small pieces of pickled daikon radish. This was our lunch.

The train carriages were of the open-plan type, with tables between each group of seats. Toilets were at both ends of each carriage and these would be in constant use throughout the journey. The toilets were similar to those we had encountered everywhere in the Far East, with no seat, just an oblong hole in the floor. Guards were posted at the end of each carriage, where the doors were situated.

Alan's route on the infamous "hell ships" from Java to Japan – via Singapore, Saigon and Taiwan. Approximately 3,500 miles by sea, followed by 1,000 miles on a train to reach the ferry to Hakodate. (map based on US Military Academy mapping of 1941)

The port of Moji where the Tofuku Maru docked (1920s postcard)

Mount Fuji, close to the route taken by the train from Shimonoseki to the far north of Japan (1930s postcard)

CHAPTER SEVEN

NORTHBOUND THROUGH JAPAN: November 1942

Our train pulled out of the station in the afternoon and proceeded through the town of Shimonoseki. As the railway lines crossed over main streets without the safety of barriers, the train travelled very slowly. As a result the civilian population were able to take a very good look at their captured enemy and, as most of them had never seen Europeans before, we must have been quite a novelty. But in our current state, with our thick beards and dirty clothing, we were not a pretty sight. We then travelled the full length of the main island of Honshu, a distance of around 1,000 miles, passing through many towns where the train always slowed down to a crawl. Meals were served in "bento" boxes and consisted of rice with daikon. After three days our train eventually arrived at a ferry port (believed to be the port of Aomori) on the northern coast of Honshu, the train coming to a halt on the dockside. There we boarded a passenger ferry and were marshalled into the main lounge area which was a very large room with no seating. On either side of the main walkway, which was in the centre, there were platforms built about 18" from the floor, all covered with straw-filled interlocking mattresses which were only a few inches thick. The guards made us remove our boots and we spread ourselves on the platforms. We were not the only passengers on board and we were constantly peered at through the windows which separated us from the outdoor parts of the deck. God knows what they thought of us as we were a miserable and dirty lot by now, having not washed for three or four days and we all had unkempt beards!

The Japanese were poorly dressed. Most of the men were in a type of uniform with peaked caps which were laced up the back, plus knee-length puttees and split-toe black sandshoes which were ankle-high and fastened at the back. The women all seemed to wear the same style of baggy trousers, fastened at the ankles. The trousers hung very low around the woman's bottom – this was to accommodate the upper dress which was bunched up and tucked into the trousers. The hanging seat of their pants made their short legs look even shorter. Their shoes were open wooden sandals with built-up blocks underneath. A shawl over the head and shoulders completed their outdoor attire. Even though we had learned to recognise our guards, now being able to distinguish one from another, the group of civilians outside our windows all looked alike – apart from the fact that we knew which were men and which were women. We subsequently learned that the Japs similarly believed we all looked the same, except that our hair colour could vary whereas theirs was always black.

The ship sailed in the early afternoon and soon we were again on the open sea. The weather by now was atrocious with high winds and snow that was whipped into blizzards. We were glad to be in a warm and dry lounge and, as by now we were all good sailors, the rolling of the ship did not affect us. We could see that many of the Japanese civilians however were quite seasick. This journey from one island to the next took about three hours. We had only one meal aboard – the usual rice and daikon, served in bento boxes. This was obviously the staple food in Japan – since arriving in Moji we had eaten nothing else. Eventually, through the swirling snow, we saw lights and the ship tied up against the dockside.

It was now evening and, after the civilians had disembarked, we were ordered out on deck. Trying to collect our kit and looking for our boots took some time and the guards moved in with fists, boots and rifle butts to speed us on our way. When we arrived on deck we were counted then, everything being to their satisfaction, the guards marshalled us off the ship. The march to the camp is one I will not forget. Snow was still falling and the ground was thickly covered, making progress very difficult. The majority of us were still in thin, tropical clothing and the keen wind cut through us, numbing our joints. As we trudged along, carrying our belongings, we began to warm up. It took about an hour to reach the camp where we were again counted. This took another 15 minutes.

After we had settled in, a meal was served and we found lumps of pork fat floating in the soup that accompanied the bowl of rice. During the nine months we had been prisoners, we hadn't seen meat so this pork fat was indeed a treat. After our meal, the lights were switched off with only two bulbs remaining lit in the corridor. After the long journey and the march to camp, we were all worn out so it did not take long to drop off to sleep.

CHAPTER EIGHT

HAKODATE CAMP: December 1942

We were now on the island of Hokkaido, the most northern and coldest of Japan's islands. The town where our camp was located was Hakodate, at the southern tip of the island. The camp was about two miles from the town, perched on a steep hillside overlooking the bay. Above us the hill was covered with a forest of pine trees and the bay was surrounded by mountains. The scene was beautiful, reminiscent of the Scottish highlands.

The camp consisted of a collection of long wooden huts surrounded by an eight foot high fence with double gates. Just inside these gates was the Jap guardhouse and their living quarters. Next was a store room building with a sentry box on its roof. After that, the next building was a bathhouse, which was raised higher than the other buildings to accommodate the large, square bath. The wooden floor of the bathhouse was open-slatted. When we bathed, we stood naked outside the bath and used small wooden basins to ladle water out of the bath, then soaped and rinsed ourselves off. Only then were we allowed to soak in the hot bath which was about 3 feet deep and could take about 20 people at any one time. The surplus soapy and dirty water drained through the slatted floor on to the sloping ground and disappeared down the hillside towards the bay below. Adjoining our bathhouse was the Japanese bath, separated from ours by a wooden partition. This was used by the guards, their officers, and all the staff including female clerks and typists. Both sexes bathed together – we heard that the civilian population also bathed together in groups at public baths.

Next to the bathhouse was the cookhouse, staffed by 12 POWs who worked in two shifts. This was a plum job which everyone wanted – we all envied the cooks who were working there. The equipment used was two large iron bowls (resembling upturned helmets) – these were set into a brick-built range with a fire grate underneath. There was also an upright oven with tin trays. Facing the bathhouses were the administration buildings with a parade ground, and facing the store room were the Jap officers' quarters. The sick bay adjoined the administration offices.

Our living quarters were single storey huts made entirely of wood. The interior of my hut was divided into eight small rooms – compartments with sliding doors made of thin slats and paper. There were eight men in each room. A wide corridor ran the full length of the building. Straw-filled thin mattresses covered the wooden floors inside each room – the mattresses were only 2" thick. All boots and shoes had to be taken off and left outside the room. There was no heating in the rooms, just two pot-bellied stoves in the corridor (one at either end), with metal flue pipes going out through the roof. Under the pitched roof, the ceilings of the rooms were about 7 feet high and were made from large squares of plywood joined by wooden beading. The ceiling void was to come in handy for concealing contraband goods that we would later acquire. Toilets and washrooms were at the end of each hut. All the electric wiring was outside the buildings, running under the eaves, protected by only a cloth covering.

This was our new abode at the beginning of December 1942. It offered only the minimum essentials required to live in the sub-zero temperatures we were experiencing.

The guards who had accompanied us to Hakodate had now left and we were at first in the charge of guards who were back in Japan after being involved in action in the war zones. Most of them were alright but, as in any group, there is always a bad one. Also the commander of guards was a bully. On many occasions we were given a good beating for talking after lights out, and at other times for being late at morning tenko. When the guard commander, who was only of Private 1st Class rank, was off duty we had no problems with any of the guards – they would stop and talk about their families and children.

We settled into the routine of our new camp and, as we did not have any work during the first few weeks, we spent our time around the stoves trying to keep warm. A sewing centre was set up and all extra blankets were cut and converted into battle blouses for the men who were still dressed in tropical kit. We also set up a cobbler's room where boots were repaired from any worn-out footwear we could find. Our cooks were chosen by the Japs and started work, preparing meals with the rations that were provided daily. These consisted of rice three times a day, with the portion per person being a small mug of rice packed very loosely, plus a mug of soup made from stock from horse bones boiled until they became so soft that they disintegrated. This added body to the liquid, in which pieces of daikon floated. During these first few weeks, I had my first dose of stomach problems. Having had a trouble-free time on the journey from Singapore, I spent several days and nights running to the toilets. I now knew how the chaps with dysentery were suffering. My problem lasted about seven days then cleared up. Others were less fortunate and continued their daily and nightly treks for much longer.

One day towards the end of this spell of yasume, we were all called out on parade. There we met our Jap commandant who, because his perpetual self-satisfied grin resembled a famous cartoon character cat of the period, was nicknamed "Felix". Despite the grin, he turned out to be a sadistic sod. He spoke only Japanese and gave us a lecture which was then translated by the Jap interpreter. In essence the message was that we were there to work hard and obey all commands given by the Jap officers and guards. He then ordered us to march past him and salute. This we did in the normal British fashion but he wanted a goose-step type of marching. Nobody would do this so we were kept there, marching up and down all morning, but still we would not goosestep. Eventually Tom Glassbrook, a sergeant of RAF 605 Squadron who was in charge of the parade and in peril of being beaten up because of our disobedience, managed to persuade "Felix" that the British forces did not goosestep but marched to attention instead. When Felix saw that this was all we would do, he agreed. So we marched past him to attention, giving him the salute he demanded. After we had fallen out and returned to our billets, we were informed by the cookhouse that there would be no lunch that day – a punishment for not following orders. This was our introduction to Felix the camp commandant.

We still had our beards as we had not shaved since leaving Changi. Felix now gave orders that we had to shave off all facial whiskers but of course he didn't say with what, nor did the Japs issue any razor blades. There was quite a queue outside any rooms where there were scissors and, after having our beards trimmed with these, the search was on for razors. As some of the older hands had cutthroat razors and were prepared to share these, we were all able eventually to parade for inspection clean-shaven. Many of us had cuts and nicks through the use of unfamiliar razors. I had used an ordinary knife which I sharpened on a piece of stone until it was sharp enough to scrape away the whiskers – as we had no soap, scrape was indeed the operative word.

Next morning we paraded at 7.30am, ready for work. Reveille had been at 6am with tenko at 6.30am, followed by breakfast and the issue of rice for our lunchtime meal. The weather was getting steadily worse with the snow about 1 foot deep. But for an issue of Japanese army clothing, we would have frozen – we had been given a pair of trousers, jacket, cap and duffle coat. These, together with our own boots and ankle puttees, made up our outdoor attire. There were 100 of us fit for work and we were first counted then marched out of the camp in columns with guards at the front, the rear and on both sides of the columns. We marched down the hillside and through the town of Hakodate, where the civilians stopped to stare at us. With a blizzard blowing they did not stay very long, we also noticed that they were quite frightened of their soldiers and scared stiff of the kempeitai. We eventually arrived at the naval shipyard – this was to be our place of work.

Hakodate town and bay (1930s postcard)

At the shipyard we were divided into groups and were in the charge of civilian "hanchos" (foremen) to do various jobs in the yard. These were jobs such as joinery, metal bending, welding, boiler making and painting. There were ten of us in my group and our hancho was an officious little man whose name was Saito. He had the customary closely cropped black hair and sported a Hitler-style moustache. He was dressed in a black hip-length tunic with khaki trousers, knee-high puttees, black split-toed sandshoes and the inevitable peaked cap. Our task was to drill holes in the boilers and then screw in the long metal tubes that would carry steam. As the boilers were standing on their ends, we had to work about 30 feet from the ground on the top of the boiler. This was a precarious metal disc no more than 8 feet in diameter, into which we had to drill the hole for a tap that then had two poles inserted at a right angle to the tap, enabling us to rotate poles to fully screw the tap into the hole. This took about two hours per hole and was monotonous work. After completing the top end, we transferred to the bottom which also needed to be drilled and tapped. We then screwed in tubes linking top and bottom together. This work was to last about 10 days and our hancho almost burst a blood vessel trying to make us go faster. The more he ranted and raved, the slower we went but, as the hanchos were allowed to beat us for not working, we were always in trouble. Working with us we had four or five young Japanese girls who oiled the taps to keep them cool and easier to turn. As they had never seen Europeans, we were quite a novelty. Once they were used to us being there, they would chat about home, family and children. They brought us small amounts of sugar and rice but, if they were caught giving us anything, they received a beating from the hanchos and guards. We were most grateful to these girls for their presents of food. At break times we ate our rice and the Japanese ate their meals with us. Their food wasn't much different to ours except they had white rice and accompaniments such as dried fish, squid or tuna. They did not eat much meat.

Our first day of work passed very slowly and, after the march back to camp through the deep snow which covered the roads, we just managed to have a bath before the evening meal was dished out. It was the usual rice and soup but, after our working day, it was not enough to satisfy our hunger. We then had about an hour before tenko and lights out. Discussing our day, Joe said he had been in a group that had been bending lengths of metal sheeting and that they worked on a giant metal pegboard raised above the floor – to bend the metal they were given a template of hardboard then their hancho drew in chalk on the pegboard the shape they had to create. As these sheets were about 1" thick the only way to bend them was to light a charcoal fire under the pegboard and place the sheets over the fire. Heavy metal pegs were then placed in the board and, when the sheets were hot enough, Joe and the rest of the group had to use sledgehammers to shape the sheets around the pegs. They continued to beat the metal and, by moving the pegs, managed to mould the sheets into the shape required. This was extremely hard work for fit men but, in our weak state, using a sledgehammer for nine hours was exhausting and half of this group could hardly march back to the camp at the end of the day.

Next morning, after tenko and breakfast, we paraded again but this time there were only 70 men ready to go to work, the balance being either camp workers or on sick parade. The Japs were furious that there was such a high proportion of men reporting sick and the Jap medical orderly went along the sick row, checking what was wrong with each person. As he proceeded along the row, unless the person had visible signs of sickness such as beri-beri where the feet and legs were swollen, they were turfed out of the sick row and put on the working party. This was to be the pattern throughout our period of captivity.

After 15 days of hard work we were allowed one day of rest, a yasume day. We could just relax, or play cards, or catch up on our laundry. Clothes were washed in cold water (when it wasn't frozen) without soap, and the wet clothes were then beaten against a stone wall in the hope that it would remove the dirt and sweat. Drying clothes was a problem during the winter but we managed by hanging them in relays over the pipes that were the chimneys from our stoves – although doing this regularly resulted in the clothes getting scorched.

The Japanese administrative staff were made up of Felix the commandant, two lieutenants (Takahashi who spoke English quite well, and Saito who spoke no English at all), a sergeant or "gunso" also called Saito (who was as mad as a hatter) and the soldiers who guarded us. Clearly Saito was a very common name in Japan. There were frequent fire drills and we had to appoint a "fire guard" to patrol the hut during the night – he was not allowed to sit. This was accomplished with a rota of one hour per man. The fire guard needed to report to the Jap guard that all was well, at the same time confirming how many men were sleeping in the hut. We had to do this in Japanese and, if we made a mistake, the guards took delight in beating us. We learned the necessary vocabulary in record time.

After a couple of months working in the shipyard, I was transferred from boiler-making to work in a gang riveting steel plates on a ship that was under construction. The gang consisted of four POWs and two Japanese girls. The girls heated the rivets in a charcoal fire until they were red hot, then a POW equipped with a large pair of tongs threw the rivet to another POW who caught it in a tin can on a pole. He placed the hot rivet in a hole in the steel plate and the final two POWs hammered home the rivet, one using a rivet gun powered by compressed air, the other using a "dolly" to hold the rivet head steady. As none of us had done this type of work before, on the first day we made a total mess of the job and were given a good beating. We soon learned to do the job to the satisfaction of the Japs. This work was more interesting than the endless drudgery of boiler-making, where the day consisted mainly of walking round in a circle pushing a pole attached to a tap. However it was more dangerous as we were working in snow, balanced on narrow planks roped to the side of the ship – there was very little room for manoeuvre when you failed to catch a stray hot rivet. Some of these missed rivets resulted in burns to our hands and bodies.

After we had riveted the plates, the Jap hancho would come along and inspect our work. This he did with a hammer, tapping the rivets to check that they rang true, in the same manner as a railway worker tapping the wheels of a carriage. He would generally find several faulty rivets which he marked with chalk to be chiselled out next day. However we discovered that, if we painted these with white lead paint, when the paint dried some of the faulty rivets passed inspection. As the painters were following us, painting the steel plates, we were able to leave quite a few useless rivets!

This work in the dockyard continued for the next six months and by then we were more organised. Joe was still bending metal on the pegboard, Jack was using an acetylene torch to cut up the metal sheeting, and I was still with the riveting gang. We shared anything we could pick up in the way of food, however there was little to steal and in any case we were searched.

The weather over the past five months had been atrocious with heavy snow. As we were even further north than Vladivostok, the biting winds came direct to us from Siberia, bringing blizzard conditions. On some mornings, when the door was opened, all that could be seen was a wall of snow which had to be dug away before we could get out of the hut. All supplies to the camp were brought in by horse and sledge as this was the only transport that could negotiate the treacherous roads. The Japs had only one thought in their heads – to get as much work as possible out of their prisoners, regardless of the consequences. Their ruling was "no work, no eat" – this meant that if only 100 men reported for work, then 100 rations would be allocated to the cookhouse for distribution. The allocation of 100 rations then had to be shared out amongst all the men, meaning even smaller amounts of food per person. As the weather grew colder, so the workforce dwindled and the rations became smaller. After our time in the tropics, with the heat and the sunshine, the rapid transition to the harsh weather of Hakodate had resulted in a trebling of the number of sick. This, coupled with the shortage of food, was dragging everyone's spirits down.

The first death in Hakodate was from amoebic dysentery. This came just a few days after we had arrived at the camp and was the start of many deaths from dysentery and colitis. As a result, we had our first taste of cremation Japanese-style. The body was placed in a small barrel in a squatting position with the knees bent and the head pushed down between them. This had to be done before rigor mortis set in. When the lid was closed the barrel was placed in a type of sedan chair with curtains covering the windows. Four men then carried this hearse, using the poles that were attached to it. It was carried out of the gates and up the hill that overlooked the camp. About 800 yards up the road, the barrel was removed and placed on a metal trolley which was then wheeled into the furnace. After a short time in the furnace, the trolley was pulled out, red hot. Some ashes which had been left to cool down were then placed in a small wooden box about 8" square. The box was then sealed with a square of paper as a lid, and given to us for burial. We had previously wondered where the strange-looking vans with curtains on the windows had been going when they passed the camp gates on their way up the hill. Now we knew that all the dead of Hakodate were cremated up there. These vans were nicknamed "baker's vans".

The ship which we were helping to build was nearing completion and, as this was a naval shipyard, we now had a visit from the Japanese navy to inspect the ship, a small "sub chaser". The launch was duly carried out and, when we left work that evening, the ship was tied up alongside the slipway. When we returned next day, it had gone. We didn't know whether it was towed away during the night or sank due to our poor work! Little did we know that this was to be our last day working in the naval dockyard for, when we cleared up for the night and were marched back to camp, nothing was said. But the next morning, when we paraded for work, there was a group of five Japanese civilians with the guards and we were broken up into parties of 20 men. A new stage in our lives had been reached.

Continued in Chapter Ten
(Chapter Nine describes the camp guards)

Satellite image showing the site of the former Hakodate POW camp, this being the green strip from bottom left to top right. A short road spur, marking the entrance to the main camp, is circled. The one remaining building (top right), originally a quarantine station constructed in 1885 during a cholera epidemic, is now a teashop/café. The grey areas in the lower part of the image, on both sides of the road, are parts of the municipal cemetery – this road leads to the crematorium. Although sited on a steep hillside high above the bay, the camp itself was on relatively flat ground. The site is about 1½ miles south west of the port, on the western slopes of Mount Hakodate.

CHAPTER NINE

THE CAMP GUARDS

Most of our army guards were now replaced by civilians who had been invalided out of the forces by being wounded or shell-shocked. We discovered almost immediately that these men had a grudge against us and intended to work it off by making our life a misery. As time went by, we found out all their nasty habits and each of these guards was given a nickname. One of them eventually even answered to, and liked his – this was Saito, a proper bastard whose favourite trick was to kick into the legs of all the sick who had leg ulcers from beri-beri, causing them terrible pain and bleeding. Someone called him "Billy Bennett" (a stage act in the 1930s who was billed as "almost a gentleman") – the name stuck and, as he was anything but a gentleman, from then on he was known to all of us as Billy Bennett.

Another guard who spoke some English was named "Yah Yah" because everything we asked him or told him would invariably result in him saying "yah yah" before answering. He was not of the same religion as most of the Japs but professed to be Christian – I don't know whether or not this was true but I do know he was a sadist who took pleasure in using the butt of his rifle as a club. I remember the first Christmas in Hakodate, after requesting that the Catholics amongst us be permitted to hold a service, they had allowed a Japanese priest into the camp to celebrate Mass. The only stipulation was that we were not allowed to converse with the priest and that a guard had to be present during the service. We agreed and the guard was our old friend Yah Yah who, though professing to be a Christian, sat through the whole service with his cap on and his rifle and bayonet held rigidly in front of him – he hadn't a clue what was going on – some Christian! That was the only Roman Catholic service we had during 3½ years of captivity as the Japs would not allow any further contact with priests from outside the camp.

There was also "Yankee Clipper", a guard who was out of the ordinary – he was about 6 feet tall and built like a barn door. He had been a boxer at some time in the Philippines and an American had given him a rough time in the ring before knocking him out. He hated all Yanks and took great delight in beating them all up. Thus the name.

We called another guard "Tenko Charlie" as he delighted in ringing the bell for evening tenko, then charging up and down the corridors of our huts, shouting at the top of his voice "tenko, tenko, all men, tenko". He would give us a kick or two to help us on our way – he was a menace at tenko time. Then there was "Minerai Charlie", a fussy little man whose rifle and bayonet were bigger than him. As we had to kick off all boots and shoes before walking into our rooms (to keep the straw mattresses clean), all footwear had to be left neatly in the corridor, outside the room – "minerai" appeared to be the Japanese word for this. Now as people kicked off the flip-flops and wooden sandals that were made for use in the camp, invariably they disturbed the neatness of the line of shoes. This guard would come into the corridor and yell to the occupants of a room to minerai their shoes. Sometimes he would even kick them out of line to get us to replace them tidily, giving us a kick or two whilst we were putting them straight. On one occasion he had caught us out two or three times during the night, disturbing our sleep. We thought we would teach him a lesson so, after lights out, we collected all of our items of footwear and took them into the room, leaving nothing in the corridor. During the night I was on fire guard when Minerai Charlie came through the door. I bowed to him and told him all was well and how many men were in the hut, at which point he turned around and noticed that all the footwear had disappeared. I thought he was going to have a heart attack as he exploded into yells of rage. I beat a quick retreat into the room, leaving him prancing up and down the corridor yelling and shouting. We were all called out and made to stand there as he went up and down the line looking for the ringleaders. Then all the "shinpans" (fire guards) were called forward and the eight of us who were guarding the fires on an hourly basis that night were each given a good punching for not having the footwear on show. Eventually he worked off his anger and allowed us to return to our rooms, after first making sure that we had placed our footwear neatly outside the rooms. However, as we had caused him to lose face, and in his eyes had humiliated him, he never forgave us and we always had to watch our step when he was around.

On another occasion one of the POWs from another room called "Shorty" had been caught talking after lights out and the guard called him out into the corridor and made him stand to attention as he proceeded to slap him across the face. Anyone caught doing anything wrong had to submit to this type of beating, without flinching or being knocked over for, if you ducked or pulled your head back, then you received a double dose of punches. If you were knocked down and didn't immediately get up, then you were really in trouble, for that was when the Japs showed their brutality by kicking you as hard as they could in the head and stomach until you had been rendered senseless. As the guard lashed out at Shorty, he held his rifle and bayonet in the other hand, with the butt on the floor and the bayonet uppermost. The first blow caught Shorty on the side of his face and, as the guard swung at him again, he instinctively pulled his head away and the guard's hand landed on the top of the bayonet with such force that it penetrated his hand. The pain must have been intense for the Jap screamed his head off and, when he pulled his hand away from the bayonet, blood spurted in all directions. By this time the guardhouse had heard all the commotion and despatched a guard to see what was happening. When he saw his compatriot with blood all over his hand he wrapped it up with a sweat towel (all the guards carried these) and, after being told that Shorty was to blame, grabbed him and marched him off to the guardhouse.

We rather thought that this would be the end for Shorty as we knew how vicious the guards could be, especially in a group. We didn't hold out much hope for poor Shorty. When we paraded next morning, he was brought out and had been given a good beating. Nevertheless they said he was fit for work but was given only a small ball of rice for his lunch. We were not allowed to share food with him as he had a guard with him but we did manage to give him the odd thing whilst we were working. When work was finished and we arrived back in camp, Shorty was immediately taken into the guardhouse and put back in the cells. As we dispersed back to our huts after being dismissed, we passed the guard who had bayoneted his hand and he had it bandaged and in a sling.

When we saw Shorty the next day, his rice ration was the same as ours and he had cigarettes with him. As he was now allowed to mingle with us, he told us a strange story. After arriving at the guardhouse on that first night, he had indeed been beaten up. Arriving back from work the next day, the first person he saw in the guardhouse was the guard with the damaged hand. The guard came over to him and, instead of the punch that Shorty was expecting, put his hand in his pocket and pulled out a packet of 10 cigarettes which he presented to him. Shorty was flabbergasted and accepted the cigarettes with a grateful "arigato" (thank you) and got into his cell. Later he was called out and taken up to the cookhouse – there he collected the meals for the guards which he carried back to the guardhouse. He was given rice and soup from their rations.

For the next seven days he received the same treatment and, apart from being locked in a cell at night, his treatment and his food were better than ours. After seven days, Shorty was returned to his hut and the guard, who still had his hand bandaged and in a sling, came to see him. Putting his good arm around Shorty's shoulders, he called him his "tomodachi" or friend. It transpired that, after hurting his hand, the guard had been put on light duties with very little to do. He attributed his good fortune to Shorty who was now his good friend. No wonder we could never fathom what the Japs were thinking, or how they were going to react to any situation!

Most of our free time was spent either talking about food and what we intended to do after the war, or playing cards. Some of the men had bridge tournaments running. We also played brag, pontoon and poker for cigarettes as these, together with rice, were the main exchange currency. We had one Jap guard who was mad on poker – of course we named him "Poker Charlie". When he was on duty he would often sit in on a poker game, giving his rifle and bayonet to someone to hold (and keep a look-out on the doors leading into the corridor). On some occasions he would be so engrossed in the game that he needed to be reminded it was tenko time – he would even get one of us to ring the bell then, at the last minute, when the Jap officer and guard commander were approaching the hut, the poker school would have to scatter to their rooms, with Poker Charlie grabbing his rifle so that he could meet his officer with a smart salute. He was never caught out and resumed playing after tenko was over, until lights out. He was quite liberal with his cigarettes and really played because he liked the card game rather than for what he could win.

Another guard nicknamed "Four Eyes" was as slimy as anything you could imagine. He was a gangly type, much taller than the usual Japs, with a sharp ferret-like face adorned with large horn-rimmed glasses. He would regularly try to ingratiate himself with us by being as nice as possible but then anything we said or did would be reported back to his superiors. It didn't take us long to find him out and either keep out of his way or not discuss anything in front of him.

Another menace was Sgt Saito (Saito-gunso) although we didn't see much of him in our living quarters, except at tenko time. He would have us out on the parade ground every morning before work, snow or shine, doing physical exercises. If you didn't put enough vigour into it, he would call you out to the platform and make you exercise in front of everyone. Whilst you were doing your arms stretch etc, he would chop away with his samurai sword, swinging it inches from your head and arms. I speak from experience – one cold miserable morning at about 6.30am when we were on the parade ground, I was towards the rear and just going through the motions without any enthusiasm when Saito came up behind me and, with a mad scream and a slap across the ear, hauled me up to the front. He began to chop around with his sword as I did the exercises with as much energy as I could. Even on such a cold morning the sweat poured off me, mostly I think with fear as Saito's sword whistled past my head and face – thank God he was an expert with that damned sword! He also liked to show off his prowess with jujutso and was always challenging us to spar with him. Only once did someone take him on and, after throwing a straight left at him, the chap was sent flying over Saito's shoulder in a move similar to a wrestler's flying mare. No one else had a go after that.

Hakodate Port (1920s postcard)

The POW camp was on a shelf of land high above the bay. This view, looking south west from the intersecting road (see satellite image on page 70), shows the site as it appears today. The camp's entrance gates would have been at the end of the tarmac road spur, with the camp stretching well beyond the trees seen in the middle distance.

CHAPTER TEN

KAIRAK

Kairak was the name of a company specialising in the hiring out of stevedores and other workers both male and female to load and unload any type of cargo from ships and barges, and to work anywhere labour was required. The five civilians we first saw at the camp were hanchos for this company and it was their job, together with the guards, to achieve the maximum amount of work by any means possible. They were all dressed identically: black jacket buttoned up to the neck, khaki jodhpur-type trousers, knee-high puttees, black split-toed sandshoes and the usual peaked cap. Each carried a bamboo cane which we were to find was used to lash out, should they be provoked in any way.

We marched off to Hakodate but instead of turning towards the shipyard, we carried on and finally arrived at a jetty on the dockside. There we were herded on to two small boats which each carried 50 men plus the guards and hanchos. We were ferried on these boats across the bay where we disembarked after a rough journey in torrential rain. We were soaked but, needless to say, the Japs had all been in the wheelhouse where it was warm and dry. Our job for the day was to unload a small fishing ship. When the fish, mainly cod and herring, was unloaded in baskets from the ship, Japanese women packed them in layers of salt in large wooden boxes then nailed on the lids. These boxes of fish weighed around 50 kg and our job was to take them from the quayside, across the road to a building which was an ice store. A lift ran up the outside of the building which was several storeys high. The boxes were placed on the lift and unloaded at doors on each storey. They were then carried into refrigerated rooms, stacked up to the ceiling and left to freeze. We called this building the "Ice Box".

When we arrived, the Japanese women were carrying boxes of fish to the ice store on wooden cradles which were strapped to their backs, supported with shoulder straps, rather like a rucksack. We had 5 gangs, each of 20 men, and took over the job of carrying these boxes. Some opted to use the same technique whilst others carried them on their shoulders – both ways were exhausting. The Japanese dockers, who lifted the boxes, were sturdy little men – they just dumped the boxes on our backs. If you had a cradle, unless you leaned forward to compensate for the weight being suddenly dumped on your back, you overbalanced and fell on your back, with the box breaking open and scattering fish everywhere. For this you received a damn good hiding with fists, feet and sticks. When you did get the box on the cradle you staggered across to the lifts and waited for the Japs to take it off your back – God, it was hard work! The weather was atrocious and we were soaking wet. Time went very slowly and, by the time we knocked off for lunch, we were physically exhausted. Our lunch was the usual small box of cold rice but, when the Japanese women saw how little we had, they shared their meagre rations with us.

After a lunch break of 30 minutes we were again at work. This time I dispensed with the back cradle and carried the boxes on my shoulder. After carrying for an hour or so, I found that the edge of the boxes was cutting into my shoulder and, as none of us had much surplus flesh, I tried padding my jacket with straw but this didn't help very much as the weight of the box pressed the straw down on the shoulder. I reverted to the wooden cradle which was nearly as bad. We suffered much taunting from the dockers – they called us old women when we used the cradles as this was the way the women carried the boxes.

We worked relentlessly throughout the afternoon and, when we were finished work at 6pm we were completely shattered. The journey back over the bay was quite hazardous as it was now dark and small boats such as ours were not easily seen. We were soaked by the waves coming into the boat and were glad to reach the landing stage. After the usual fiasco of being counted, we started off for camp, arriving there about 7pm with one mad rush to get down to the bathhouse. After the evening meal we settled down for our usual discussion and, as I had been given a cigarette by one of the women workers, we had a smoke – the cigarette was passed around and all got at least one drag out of it. We all slept well that night as we were exhausted.

On the third day we again paraded for work and marched off to the jetty. Whilst crossing the bay we noticed that we were heading in a slightly different direction and, when we landed, found ourselves on a coal wharf. We were divided into parties of seven men and taken to a railway line. There on the line was a row of railway wagons, each containing about 40 tons of coal. We were issued with shovels and our job was to unload these wagons and clear the line of coal so that the empty wagons could be shunted away. Joe, Jack and I had teamed up with another four men and we organised our group with three on top of the wagon and the other four working down on the ground. First we turned a wheel on the front of the wagon, this opened the flaps on both sides and, with the three on top pushing the wet coal through the flaps, we cleared the wagon of coal. Next we needed to clear the coal from the wheels and the line (which involved some of us crawling under the wagons). When we stopped for lunch our faces and clothes were filthy.

Lunch was taken in a wooden hut on the wharf. A metal stove was in the centre of the hut and we stoked this up with driftwood and, of course, we were not short of coal to top it up! By the time we had finished our lunch the stove was so hot that all our clothes had dried on us and we were ready to face work once again. As some of the gangs had not completed the task of clearing the coal from under the wagons, we all had to pitch in and help clear the track as the engine was due to haul the empty wagons away. The coal then needed to be moved to its storage dump. After that it was time to board the boats for our return to camp. Once again this was hazardous, this time because we had to cross the route of the passenger ferry which was just leaving its berth. We could see that the ferry was now steering straight for us and, as it came nearer, the Jap at the helm of our boat finally realised that we were in danger of being run down so he swung the wheel hard over. The ferry ploughed straight ahead and we knew that we had not been seen by its crew. The Japs on our boat certainly learned some new English words – our language was choice! Having escaped being hit by the ferry, we were caught in its wake and very nearly swamped. However, after much baling out of water, we eventually made it to the jetty.

The weather by now was picking up and we frequently woke to glorious sunshine – this made life a lot easier to bear. Marching down through Hakodate to the jetty to board our boats became a pleasure. The roads on the outskirts of the town were lined with cherry trees which were now in full bloom. We were able to dispense with our winter clothing and revert back to our own tropical kit. Nevertheless, outside the camp, we did not use our short pants but kept to the lightweight long trousers with ankle puttees as the trouser legs, fastened at the bottom, made excellent receptacles for any dried rice or fish we could steal during our working day.

By now we were doing a variety of jobs and becoming more and more proficient as stevedores as the time passed. Some of the work was more fruitful, especially when we could steal food to eat whilst working (and also to smuggle back to camp to share with our sick friends). On other jobs, such as the coal wharf, salt ships and cement ships, there were no pickings to be had – just damned hard work and plenty of it. Our periods of work had also increased in length as it was now lighter in both mornings and evenings so we started earlier and finished later. We were working from 7am until 7pm with only a 30 minute break for lunch.

It was about this time that we again went to work at the cold store and, when we arrived, the cradles were there for us to use. As we had been toughened up with heavy work, some of us including Joe, Jack, Jock, Harry (an American) and I decided that no way were we going to use these – we would carry the boxes of fish on our shoulders, even if it killed us. By the time we had finished for the day, our shoulders were red raw from the box edges cutting into us. This was not helped by the salt in which the fish was packed oozing out on to our sore shoulders. Next morning we were again sent to the cold store and the same thing happened to our shoulders. This went on for three days until we had a gang of Japanese stevedores working next to us and carrying the same type of fish boxes to the lifts. We were amazed to find that their method of carrying on the shoulder was entirely different to ours. Where we carried a box tilted and rested against the head, the Japs tilted the head and made the shoulder into a broader surface. Also the shoulder was tilted outwards but we couldn't see how the box could lean outwards without falling off. We watched for some time then saw that they were using a small metal hook to hold the box steady, hooking it in one of the two wires that were around the box.

At lunch break we discussed this method and thought we would give it a try. The Japs lifting the boxes also used hooks, one small and one large. When we explained to them that we intended to carry the boxes in the same manner as their fellow stevedores, they searched around and found us some of the smaller hooks. The boxes were placed on our shoulders in the Japanese fashion and promptly fell off, nearly crippling the lifters. We tried again and managed a few steps before the boxes again crashed to the ground, bursting open and spreading the contents, causing the Jap hancho to bawl at us. Finally Joe got the knack and carried his box the full distance to the lifts. After explaining exactly how he had managed to do this, all five of us were soon carrying the boxes with just the odd mishap. Seeing us doing this, some of the others tried and we had a party of ten who could all carry the boxes with very little trouble. That evening, when we arrived back at camp, our shoulders were slightly skinned but a lot better than previously. Whilst soaking in the hot tub at the bathhouse we decided that, if possible, we would try to stick together as a team regardless of the type of work we were assigned.

We carried on working at the ice store for a further week during which time we were put on various jobs, but mostly carrying the boxes of fish. One day we were given the job of unloading small wooden boxes from a ship and the easiest way to discover what they contained was to drop one, accidentally spilling the contents! We found that the boxes contained a substance that looked like red-coloured tapioca. Now, anything we could steal and eat without being caught was a bonus and, as we couldn't take anything whilst out in the open, carrying boxes in the ship's hold was different. We were out of sight of the guards and working with Japanese stevedores who were quite happy to eat anything that had broken open. When a box broke, the stevedores picked up handfuls of the substance and proceeded to eat it so we of course grabbed a handful each and stuffed it in our mouths. We had to be quick as we needed to continue with our work, putting the boxes in a rope net which when full would be hoisted up by the winches of the ship and swung over to the dockside for unloading and carrying to the store. The substance that we were now eating was very salty and we could only eat a small amount at a time. We did however fill up our bento boxes, to eat with our rice at lunchtime. We eventually learned that this was salmon roe and that it was a delicacy in Japan. At lunchtime we shared our spoils with the rest of our group and everyone had their fill. The only problem was that we were forever at the barrel of drinking water.

Two days later, whilst working on the dockside carrying boxes of fish, I was trotting across the road which was littered with the remains of broken wooden boxes when unfortunately I stood on a piece of wood with a large nail sticking upwards. The nail penetrated the sole of my rubber sandal and drove straight into my right foot, the piece of wood then becoming attached to my sandal like a ski. I let out a yell and the box dropped off my shoulder, hitting the ground and splitting wide open, scattering the fish in all directions. The Jap hancho was furious and dived at me but, when I showed him my foot, he stopped short and went back to where the women were boxing the fish. He picked up a hammer then came back to me – I was unsure what he planned to do. He pulled the wood and nail from my sandal and, having taken the sandal off, he put my foot between his knees, rather like a blacksmith. He then proceeded to hammer the sole of my foot, starting on the outside and working in a circle towards the nail hole which, by this time, was bleeding profusely. After working around the hole for some minutes, he then hammered the hole itself and, after a few more minutes, he put my foot down and said it should be "okay-ga". He had succeeded in stopping the bleeding and, although my foot was still rather sore, I could walk on it with very little trouble. Afterwards the hancho explained that, by hammering the foot around the wound, all the poison and bad blood had been driven out and the wound was then sealed by hammering it. For the remainder of the day I was allowed to take it easy by lifting the boxes on to the others' shoulders and, when the time came to return to camp, my foot was much better. By next morning the foot was perfectly ok with just a mark where the nail had penetrated the sole. I couldn't even wangle a day off sick as there was nothing to show the Jap medical orderly!

Our work as stevedores was quite varied and, when we paraded for work each morning, we never knew what the job would be until we arrived at Hakodate docks. Of course some days were better than others. For instance, if the job entailed loading or unloading a food product of any description, we were by now becoming first-class thieves so there was the chance of acquiring something to eat. On one particular day we were all lined up with 10 of our party right at the front and, after marching down to the docks, we were split into groups of 10 or 20 and each party had a Jap guard and a hancho in charge. We had our usual group of 10, with a hancho named Kamasawa. We had been with him before – he was about 30 years old, rather tall for a Jap, and always dressed in the same uniform as the other hanchos. The problem with this particular hancho was that he was extremely unpredictable. He had such a volatile nature he could explode for the least thing done wrong, then he would lash out with his bamboo cane and not stop until he had exhausted himself. He would then revert to being a nice guy. As our group had become proficient in most types of work and, as Kamasawa was the chief hancho and had first choice of his workforce, almost invariably we had him in charge of us.

On this particular day we boarded our boat together with another party of 20 who were in the charge of a hancho nicknamed "Hammer Chops" because all his visible teeth were either coated with metal or had metal crowns – when he laughed, all that could be seen were these two rows of metal. As the launch proceeded out into the bay we realised that, instead of the usual ice store, we were making for a ship that was anchored in the harbour. We pulled alongside a companionway leading up to the deck and disembarked. The ship was a ferry which plied between the islands of Japan and was carrying a cargo of dried fish which we had to unload on to barges tied alongside. We split up into two parties with our 10 allocated to two of the barges and prepared to be lowered down on the first slings of cargo from the holds. We had to hang on to the net as it was swung over the side of the ship and lowered on to the barge by a Jap operating a winch which controlled the ship's derricks, a dicey arrangement but the only way that we could get on and off the barges. It was glorious weather and being out in the open was a treat as we had neither guards nor hanchos with us, only the two old bargees who actually lived on the barge (down in a small cabin in the bow, complete with stove and beds). The cargo of dried fish was packed into large hessian sacks which the other chaps, who were working in the ship's two holds, stacked on to the nets which were then hoisted up, swung over the side of the ship, and dropped on to the barges. We would then empty the net, stacking the sacks of dried fish on the deck of the barge. As the stacks got higher we would use wooden planks to make a series of ramps, enabling us to stack the sacks about ten tiers high. This was extremely hard work as there were only five of us working on the barge and it meant two men lifting sacks on to the shoulders of the other three who carried the sacks up the planks to the bargees who then stacked them. The only consolation was that we could eat as much dried fish as we wanted because some of the sacks "accidentally" broke open. The ship also carried dried seaweed which was edible so we took every opportunity to eat this – although it was very salty, it contained iodine which was good for us. Lunch was taken on the barges so we had plenty to supplement our rice ration. Toilet facilities on the barges were non-existent and we had to squat over the edge – just as well we had no Japanese women working with us on these occasions. Although the Japs conducted random searches after work, we still managed to smuggle dried fish and seaweed back to camp in various ways – down our trouser legs, stuffed in our packs, or up our sleeves – of course if you were caught then you got a good hiding and possibly a week in the guardhouse cells. This ferry came into Hakodate once a week and we always looked forward to unloading it.

On the other hand, we were sometimes taken out to a ship and, having looked forward to a good feed from its cargo, were left disappointed when we found that the cargo was something inedible such as salt. I recall one such period when we were shovelling salt into nets lined with pieces of hessian. This was unrelenting hard work in very hot conditions so we would strip down to the waist and, as the nets were hoisted out of the hold, salt streamed out of holes in the hessian, covering our sweating bodies. This caused a rash, leaving raw patches where the skin had rubbed away. There was no way of avoiding this as, working in such close confines, the salt sprayed everywhere. Our clothes became impregnated with salt and, when we put them on to return to camp, they felt slightly damp but not too uncomfortable. The next morning however was a different matter for overnight our clothes had absorbed all the dampness from the night air and were wet. On misty mornings, we had to wring out the water before putting our clothes on. At least we had boxes of salt to help add flavour to our boiled rice!

All the barges that we loaded had to be towed in and unloaded into the warehouses that lined the dockside. Therefore, after spending two days loading the barges, we then spent a further three or four days unloading them. We had working with us on the barge five or six Japanese girls who filled sacks – these sacks of salt were then weighed on a scale. Two of us would then lift the sacks on to the shoulders of the others in our gang, they then carried the sacks into the warehouse. Joe and I worked together lifting the sacks, working with the same girls. We got to know them quite well and they asked us about our homes, families and whether we had wives and children. I was 20 or 21 years old and Joe a year older than me, neither of us was married. When the girls asked us in sign language by lifting a little finger whether we had a wife, we told them no. Then we asked if they had a husband, this time raising a thumb (again this was Japanese sign language) as this seemed to be their main topic of conversation. One girl indicated that she was married with one child and we said that, although we had no wives, we each had three children. They were poleaxed and went into a huddle giggling. During lunch they gathered all their friends and told them about "our children" – Joe and I had become celebrities. They kept coming over to us and checking how many children we had, but without a wife. We never did tell them that we had been kidding!

On one occasion our group was unloading a barge full of salt, with the usual Japanese girls working with us, when we noticed that the barge tied alongside us had a cargo of wooden boxes which, from experience, we knew contained tins of fish. We decided to have a couple of boxes for ourselves. When the barges were brought into the wharves for unloading they were always tied up with the stern nearest to the dock and the bow facing out into the bay. This made unloading easier as the deck at the stern end was open and planks could be laid from it, straight on to the shore. When we arrived and started working, the tide was out and the barges were lying in the mud. We checked that the guard was out of sight and, after explaining to the girls what we had planned, Joe nipped over the side of our barge on to the other one and passed two of the boxes to me. I dumped these on the deck and covered them with salt. Joe and I continued to lift sacks of salt on to the shoulders of the rest of the group then, after getting Jack and Jock to take over, we broke open the boxes with shovels. We took out all the tins and made sure that all the wood from the boxes was carried away in the sacks of salt. There were enough tins to give everyone including the girls three tins apiece (they would take theirs home, concealed in their bags – these were never searched). When the salt was shovelled into the sacks, we placed three tins on the top, buried just below the surface, and when the sack was carried in to the warehouse, each man had to request a toilet break to open the tins. This was accomplished with the metal hooks that we used for holding the sacks. After eating the lot, the empty tins were buried in the salt. We took it in turns and eventually cleared our stash of tins – they contained crayfish which tasted marvellous!

This is the only building that remains. Prior to becoming a POW camp in 1942, it is believed that this part of the site (including this building) was used as an isolation sanitorium for tuberculosis patients.
Photos: Azusa Matsumoto (taken before 2006 renovation)

CHAPTER ELEVEN

DAILY LIFE AND DEATH

The camp was now well-organised and the Japs had been persuaded to let us keep a couple of pigs and a cow. The pigs were a boar and a sow we planned to breed from. The cow was to provide milk – we told the Japs that it would help to get sick people back to work. One of our men, a farm hand in civilian life, was detailed to look after the animals and milk the cow each day. The cow produced four buckets of milk per day, three of which were used to supplement the rations of the sick, the other bucket was shared out on a rota basis, giving one cup of milk every two or three weeks. When the sow had piglets we planned that the meat would also be shared out but only one piglet was used in this way, the rest being sold by the Japs to an outside butcher.

On one occasion there was a stillborn piglet and the Japs said we could have it to put in the soup. It was taken to the cookhouse and cut into pieces but instead of using it in our rations the cooks switched it with the Japs' ration of pork. Meat from the stillborn piglet must have been ok as none of the guards took ill.

It was a great occasion in the camp when the pig was killed and it was done on a yasume day when all were there to help. A large tripod was erected using tree trunks about 8 feet long, the tops being lashed together with ropes, then a fire was lit alongside and a large cauldron (borrowed from the cookhouse) was filled with water and placed on the fire to boil. The pig was then driven from its pen (which was down beside the guardhouse for security reasons) by a crowd of us, with much whooping and shouting. We drove it up to the area where it was to be killed, where it was secured with ropes around its feet. Then, using a sledgehammer, one of the butchers killed it with a blow to the head and it was hoisted up on the tripod by its back feet. When the rope was secured, the pig's throat was cut open and the blood was collected in a large ladle and taken to the cookhouse to be used to flavour the soup. When all the blood had drained out, the butchers set to work scraping off the hair with hot water and knives, after which the pig was completely skinned (the Japs used pigskin for making the uppers of their boots). When this had been completed the carcass was cut down and carried to the cookhouse where the butchers cut it up using every scrap. It was said that the only thing not used for food was the grunt! The Japs of course took the major part (and the best cuts) but our soups for the next week or so were rich with pieces of pork and fat floating in them. The toilets were never busier, for the pork fat gave the majority of us the runs – but it was worth it.

Deaths from dysentery, beri-beri and malnutrition were still occurring. These were very sad occasions, when we had to take the bodies of our friends up to the crematorium and bring back their ashes. But life had to go on and, even though we were depressed after anyone died, we had to keep hoping that we would survive and that our captivity would not last too long. We had now been prisoners for about 15 months and the death rate, although slowing down, was still something we had to contend with. Beri-beri is an ailment caused by the lack of Vitamin B. In our case this was caused by eating polished white rice and not having fresh fruit or vegetables. The main symptom is that extremities such as toes, feet, fingers and hands start to swell up with water. When the skin is pressed, the hollow dent stays there and the sensations of touch and pain disappear. Without treatment, the swelling continues up the arms and legs, making them swell so much that trousers, shirts and jackets cannot be worn – the only thing to wear is a sarong or towel wrapped around the waist. Shoes or boots are also impossible. The sufferer becomes very unsteady and cannot balance properly. When lying down, every movement is accompanied by a gurgling sound as the water in the body moves around. If the beri-beri is not treated, the water reaches the heart and the patient effectively drowns in his own juice. A simple remedy was to take tablets made from the crushed husks of the very rice that we were being fed. But the Japs did not supply us with these tablets, nor did they give us the greens that we needed. The result was that men died needlessly. Beri-beri was obvious to the Jap medical orderly when he went down the line looking for signs of illness, therefore sufferers were excused work detail – which was just as well as they could not get their pants on.

I can speak with some authority on the subject of beri-beri as I was one of the unfortunate people to contract this. The first I knew of it was when my fingers started to swell up, then my toes. At first I thought I had caught frostbite but as the days passed, I found that my boots were getting harder to put on, my ankles had swollen and I was constantly thirsty. I reported sick but the Jap medical orderly would not let me stay off work because I could still walk. Therefore I had to go out each morning in the certain knowledge that, by the time I returned, my limbs would have swollen a bit more. This went on for a week and by then my legs had swollen so much that I could only wear a towel wrapped around me. The Japs then allowed me to stay in camp, officially sick. One day, whilst sitting by the stove, I tried to get up when one of the guards came into the hut. Everyone had to stand to attention and bow whenever a Jap appeared and, as I was bowing, I found that I had lost my balance and was falling. I put out my right hand to grab something and the only thing solid was the stove which was exceedingly hot. However I couldn't feel anything and the first time I realised that my hand was burning was when one of the others pulled it off the side of the stove. My palm (where I had been grasping the stove) was red raw and, as I looked at it, blisters started to cover it. The guard took me to the hospital hut and I had a bandage put on the burn.

That evening we received a postcard to write home and, as I found it impossible to write, one of my friends had to do so, explaining what had happened – this card duly arrived home and was kept for my return. My limbs continued to swell up with water, which was impossible to get rid of. There was no pain, in fact a knife could be stuck into your hand and it would not hurt. After being in camp for about a month I realised that if I stayed there on the sick, I was certain to die in the same manner as some of the men who had succumbed to beri-beri. I took my trousers and split open the side seams so that I could get my legs inside. I made holes in the cloth and laced up the sides with string then, getting two pals to support me, I went out on the work detail.

That day we went to the coal wharf and all I could do was use a shovel to scoop coal away from the wagons. After working for some time I requested a trip to the toilet which was the usual benjo stuck out on two poles over the sea wall. On my way there I passed the spot where one of the guards had left his haversack containing his belongings. As anything belonging to the Japs was fair game for us to lift, I took a quick look inside and there was a bottle of quite large brown pills together with his rice ration. I stole the bottle of pills and climbed into the benjo. I bit into one of the pills which had a yeasty taste, then decided to consume the lot – about 12 pills – and dumped the bottle in the sea. I returned to my shovelling and, when we broke for lunch, I found that I had started to sweat profusely and constantly wanted to pass water. In fact the waterworks were working overtime. This continued all afternoon and, by the time we returned to camp, I had lost so much water that the swelling in my body seemed to be subsiding. By next morning, having spent much of the night in the toilet, I found that my feet and hands were almost back to normal and after a couple of days I had recovered from my beri-beri. Stealing the tablets had been a risk as I could have been caught. Eating them had been a bigger gamble but God must have been with me that day. Fortunately I did not have a relapse nor did I ever suffer from beri-beri again.

We had by now created a black market with the merchant seamen on whose ships we worked. As they were always on the lookout for clothes, boots and blankets, we offered our surplus clothing and the blankets of any men who had died. These were traded for tea, sugar and cigarettes which in turn were used in the camp as currency to purchase more clothes! Getting the clothes or blankets out didn't cause any difficulties as we wore the clothing or used the blankets as scarves. Returning with the proceeds of our day's trading was a different matter – the only way to beat the searches at the end of the working day was to pass any contraband to friends who had already been searched or to conceal any small items about the body. If caught, the punishment was a beating and a week in detention in the guardhouse. I remember one day trading a blanket for cigarettes and, on returning to camp that evening, did not have the opportunity to pass these to someone who had already been searched. As the guards drew ever nearer I was becoming more desperate by the minute and finally I took the cigarettes from my haversack and placed them under my Japanese cap. When it was my turn to be searched, I waited until the guard had been through my haversack and had checked my pockets then, grabbing the crown of the cap together with the cigarettes, I lifted up the cap and was thrilled to hear the guard say OK. Once again I had managed to outwit our captors. With the tea that we brought into camp we had to be careful as neither tea nor sugar were ever issued to us – we had to conceal these in all sorts of places to beat the frequent searches and, when we were brewing up, this had to be done surreptitiously as the guards constantly patrolled the huts. Around the pot-bellied stove we placed two wires about 12" apart and, having stripped our British water bottles down to the metal, we attached a hook fashioned from wire to the neck of the bottle. When it was filled with water, the bottle could hang on the wire around the stove – we were able to get about a dozen bottles around the stove (with the flat of the bottles resting against it) and another four or five on the top. We put one spoonful of tea in each bottle and allowed it to stew until hot enough. The tea leaves were used again and again until flavourless, then they were smoked in our pipes. We wasted nothing.

Around this time we were informed that a representative of the Red Cross would be visiting the camp therefore everything had to be cleaned up. We spent a couple of days doing this and the Japs issued further clothing for us to wear, also extra blankets. The Red Cross rep duly arrived and, dressed in a white suit, he did a quick tour of the camp accompanied by the commandant and his officers. We were not allowed to speak to him or to make any complaints – it was a complete waste of time as far as we were concerned. Nevertheless it did demonstrate that our presence in Hakodate as POWs had been noted and that our relatives should be notified of our whereabouts. The evening meal that night was a lot better with the soup containing pieces of meat and with double rations of rice. After the departure of the Red Cross rep, all the extra clothing and blankets were collected and returned to the stores. And it was back to normal rice rations and watery soup.

About a month later there was much excitement in the camp when a lorry load of wooden cases arrived and the working party unloading them had seen that they were stencilled with Red Cross markings. There were also sacks of cocoa and sugar on the lorry. Everything was unloaded into the stores hut and our anticipation grew with the passing of every day. We were kept in suspense for over a week then, after the evening meal on our yasume day, the hut orderlies were called to the cookhouse and they returned with buckets full of steaming hot cocoa already sweetened with sugar. This was rationed out at one mug per man and we queued up to get it. As we sat drinking this delicious beverage we deliberated about what other goods could be in the wooden cases locked in the Jap stores. We had to wait another week or two before the Japs decided to issue the rest of the Red Cross goods and they consisted of American Army coats and boots plus a good supply of books (for which we converted a spare room into a library) and some blocks of processed cheese, the only food sent. The cheese was issued to the cookhouse and dished out with our evening meal at about 2 ounces per man – the Japs had of course taken the majority share of this cheese before giving the balance to us. The cocoa and sugar lasted about a week – after that, it was back to the usual ration of one cup of cow's milk every two or three weeks. We were allowed to wear the boots from the Red Cross for going to work but, as these were issued only to men who went out on working parties, quite a few POWs missed out on this footwear. At least everyone could share in the use of the books from our new library and, after reading two or three books, I decided to concentrate on specific authors, reading as many books as possible. I read all the western novels by Zane Grey, then moved on to foreign legion books by P.C.Wren and others I cannot remember. One author really caught my imagination and, when I was finally released and arrived home, I bought as many of his books as I could – his name was Lloyd C. Douglas and I still enjoy reading his books over and over. I have also seen at least three films based on his books: The Robe, The Big Fisherman and Magnificent Obsession.

We were still working as stevedores and, arriving back in camp one evening, I went as usual for a hot bath before my meal. Whilst in the bathhouse washing myself down before getting into the tub for a good soak, I heard the Japs in the adjoining bathhouse (which was separated from ours by a wooden partition) having their bath accompanied by two Japanese girls who worked in the offices. There was much hilarity and one of the Jap officers popped his head over the dividing partition. He shouted that American soap was "dami dami" (no good) and threw the block of soap at us. I picked it up and realised that it was a block of the cheese from our Red Cross supplies. His loss was our gain for the cheese was washed and eaten that night!

CHAPTER TWELVE

WORK CONTINUES

Our work as stevedores brought variable rewards. One day, having become fed up unloading cement, I thought I would take a look around the ship to see if there was anything worth stealing. With the usual excuse of going to the toilet I climbed out of the hold and on to the deck. I wandered down a companionway towards the stern of the ship, looking through doors and portholes that I passed. About half way to the stern I detected the smell of bacon frying and, as I looked through the door into what must have been the galley, I saw a Jap standing beside a stove and on it was a large pan with bacon rashers sizzling away. I continued on my way and, finding that the toilets were only three doors away, I returned to the galley and this time the cook was nowhere in sight so I crept in, grabbed the pan and emptied it into my cap. Replacing the cap on my head, the bacon burning my scalp, I dashed to the toilets and wolfed down the lot. It certainly tasted good! As I made my way back to the hold I heard the Jap cook going wild but I managed to get down there to start work again. When I passed the galley later the door was tightly closed. When we finished work for the day, everyone was thoroughly searched and, as the cargo of cement wasn't worth stealing, I could only assume that they were checking whether anyone still had the stolen bacon on them – some hope of that! On the way back to the camp our guards for the day Billy Bennett and Four Eyes were very aggressive, kicking and punching us so I gathered that they had been taken to task and blamed for the bacon being stolen.

The next day we finished unloading the cement by late afternoon and, covered from head to toe in cement dust on a hot and sunny day, we asked if we could have a dip in the bay. After warning us to behave, "no men escape-o", Billy Bennett allowed us to have a swim. I could not swim but I wasn't going to miss a chance to clean off the cement dust so I jumped over the side, hanging on to a rope. After about 15 minutes we were called in and, after dressing, caught our launch back to the landing stage where we joined with others who had been working elsewhere. One of the parties had been working in a factory packing cans of salmon into cases and loading these on a barge. We decided that we would try next day to be on that particular job.

The next morning we were up early and, after breakfast and collecting our rice rations, we lined up for work hoping to wangle a job in the canning factory. After the usual rigmarole of being checked by the guards and saluting the Jap officer, we were ready to march to work. There was always a tussle to get in the first few rows as there would be more chance of spotting fag ends in the road – these were picked up to be used later for rolling our own cigarettes or for smoking in the pipes which we made from driftwood. Our usual group had stayed together and unfortunately we were sent by launch across the bay to a dirty old tramp steamer with small wooden boats stacked on the deck and lashed to it. We set to work on a barge alongside the steamer and did not know what the cargo was – taking off the tarpaulin was always like a lucky dip. This time we found sacks of charcoal and we soon became filthy dirty but had cleared these within an hour or so. The cover was turned further back and we moved to the next part of the cargo which was potatoes and cabbage. Then, with the cover turned fully back we found fishing nets and realised that the small boats we had seen on the deck of the steamer were for fishermen who spent two or three months at a time on distant small islands where the fishing grounds were good. The bargees had told us about this, and how the fish they caught were salted. Having cleared the nets we came across bags of salt. All of the cargo was transferred to the steamer. By now it was getting near lunchtime and a tugboat towed a further two barges alongside and we made a start on the cargo of one of them. The first thing we found when we rolled back the tarpaulin was a row of wooden boxes which we knew would contain some sort of tins. As we unloaded the cargo we tried to work out a plan to get ourselves some of these tins. Working in the hold of a ship always presented opportunities to break open a crate and steal some of the contents but an open barge was more difficult. Finding out how many more slings were to be hoisted before lunch, we waited until the second last sling and then carefully placed two boxes so that they would slip out of the net when it was lifted. The hook descended and I fitted it into the rings of the net and the winch man began to hoist up the load. As it lifted, the two boxes began to slip but then stopped – we thought we had blown it. However, as the net was being swung over the side of the ship, it caught a cleat and tipped, throwing not just two boxes but half the load down on to the barge. We dived in all directions as the boxes rained down on us, disgorging their contents of tinned salmon. There were cans everywhere, some of them rolling into the water and sinking. Full boxes also fell in to the water and these were also sinking. The panic of the bargees and Japs was something to behold and, while they were dashing around recovering the full boxes, we were grabbing loose tins and concealing them in our clothing and haversacks.

After the Japs had recovered the boxes from the sea they began to repair the broken crates, placing loose tins in them. We helped and, when all were repaired, found that the last box had about 30 tins missing. As the two bargees had seen tins sinking in the water they did not suspect us of taking any. At lunch, up on the deck of the ship (where we were preparing to exchange jobs with our mates who had been working on the ship while we worked on the barge), we shared our spoils. The tinned salmon went well with our boiled rice although we had to be careful as Yah Yah the guard was unsure whether we had contrived the incident. The empty tins were later disposed of among the cargo. After lunch I was working in the ship's hold with Joe, Jack, Jock and Nobby and we had two Nips working with us, checking that we were packing the hold correctly to eliminate any movement of the cargo in bad weather. There was a variety of food, clothing and other goods coming down on the slings and of course we were on the lookout for anything we could "lift". Any boxes we were unsure of would have the lids forced open to check the contents, before resealing the lid and stacking the box. Halfway through the afternoon Joe picked up a box which felt very light and found that it was packed with biscuits, something we had not seen for some time. We all had a handful, including the two Japs working with us, and put the box to one side while we continued to fill the hold. We kept eating them until we had cleared the lot, the empty box then being buried under other cargo.

After the salmon tins "accident" we were right to predict a thorough search at the end of the day. Yah Yah went through our clothes and haversacks but found nothing. When we arrived back at camp the five of us who had been working together could not eat our rice rations and passed them to our less fortunate sick friends. However the saga of this ship was far from over as we were to find out about a month later when the kempeitai arrived at the camp. The ship that we had loaded for the fishermen with food, clothing and other goods had caught fire at sea and the kempeitai were ready to claim that we had sabotaged it. They wanted to know who smoked as they were looking to blame anyone who smoked a pipe. Their case was that a pipe smoker must have knocked out the ashes in the hold and that these had smouldered until catching fire. They had narrowed the fire down as starting in a particular hold and wanted to know who had worked in it. I had not worked in the affected hold. One of those who had been working down that hold was Sgt Tom Glassbrook who was the only pipe smoker in the group. The kempeitai immediately arrested him and took him away from the camp to be charged with sabotage at a court martial hearing to be held in an army barracks in a nearby town. We didn't hear any more for about two weeks but we still had to send our working parties during this time and were very careful not to cause any trouble while Tom was in custody.

Then, arriving in camp from work one evening, the first person to greet us was Tom Glassbrook. After our meal he told us what had happened to him whilst in the custody of the kempeitai, and at the court martial. He had been held in the cells at the army barracks but treated quite well, being given the same rations as the Jap army. The trial was held in the barracks, lasting two days and conducted all in Japanese although an interpreter had been provided for him. The case for the prosecution had been made and it was stated that such an act of sabotage would incur the death penalty. Tom had asserted that no POW would knock smouldering tobacco out of his pipe as this would waste a commodity that was difficult to obtain. He also submitted evidence that, when a pipe was laid aside or placed in an enclosed space, the pipe would automatically extinguish itself. To present his evidence he had his pipe filled with tobacco by the Japs then, after lighting and smoking it for a while, he put it in his pocket for a few minutes and when taken out the tobacco was completely extinguished. The presiding officers left the room for a conference and, when they returned, they dismissed the case and Tom was returned to our camp a very happy man. After he recovered from this episode he once again joined our working parties and was quite a celebrity with the guards as none of them had any time for the kempeitai.

Although we were now very proficient as stevedores, we were occasionally sent back to the coal wharf and on one occasion we were loading coal on to the small ships that plied between the islands. The coal was carried in wicker baskets, each man having two baskets attached to a pole balanced over one shoulder. The load then had to be carried up wooden planks which had been placed across the top of the ship's hold. When over the hold, ropes attached to the bottom of each basket had to be pulled, upending the baskets and emptying the coal into the hold. Balanced on a plank 18" wide, about 20 feet above the floor of the hold, this was a dangerous job and it was important to pull the ropes simultaneously to avoid being thrown off balance. None of us had any experience of this type of work so it was going to be a long, hard day. In our group were Joe, Jack, Jock, Jimmy, Tom, Nobby, Tiny and two Americans Harry and Frank. Our hancho for the day was Hammer Chops who explained that we had to fill our own baskets with coal, have them weighed and that this weight must be at least 35 kg. We were given a wooden marker for each trip we made and this had to be handed in at the foot of the plank running up to the ship, enabling the hancho to check how many baskets of coal had been loaded. The crew supervised the loading and moved the load from side to side so that the centre of gravity was kept in the middle of the ship. There was also the plimsoll marking on the bow and we eventually worked out that, if we continued to heap the coal in the centre, it would take time for the bow mark to be brought down. This meant extra work so we learned to load as much coal as possible at the front of the hold in order to bring the bow down to the plimsoll line.

On the first day we didn't know all this and just kept carrying our full baskets all day long – until the skipper of the ship was satisfied that he had enough coal on board. Our job was then finished and we thought we would be taken back to camp. However the group working on the other ship had not completed their loading and we were informed by Hammer Chops that no one would return to the camp until the work was completed. We moaned about this but Billy Bennett, our guard, agreed with the hancho and we had to help loading the other ship. This was not finished until about 7pm and only then were we allowed to board the launch to return to camp. We arrived two hours late but the cooks hadn't been informed – our rice and soup had been left for us to collect but it was cold.

Next day we were back at the coal wharf with another two ships to load, and with Yah Yah the guard and two hanchos (Kamasawa and Saito) in charge of us. Kamasawa told us at lunch break that when we completed the loading of our ship we would be finished for the day and would be able to sit and rest in the yasume hut until the others had completed their work. We didn't believe him so we took it easy and finished about the same time as the others. Kamasawa knew that we had been coasting and was livid. He laced into us with his stick and told us that next day we would be given all the menial tasks that took time and effort. He certainly kept his word and, for the next two days, we did nothing but unload coal wagons – much harder work than loading the ships, and with guards and hanchos supervising us all day long.

The following day we were back on the wharf and decided to take Kamasawa at his word when he repeated that, if we finished the job early, we could yasume with no extra work. It was raining stair rods that day so the sooner we completed the work, the sooner we could get into the yasume hut and dry out. We set to work but it had rained heavily all night and the coal (which was partly dust) weighed very heavy. As a result the minimum weight for each basket was set at 40 kg. We soon got into our stride and worked without a break until the ship was completely loaded, trimmed and ready to sail. By now it was lunchtime and we had each shovelled and carried 10 tons of coal on to the ship, no mean feat in our emaciated state – we were certainly ready to eat. In the hut we built a fire in the central stove and the air soon warmed. We sat on apple boxes and relaxed. When the time came for resuming work, the others moved out but we sat tight and didn't move. The guard that day was Four Eyes who started to shout and push us. Still we didn't move and, as two or three of us had been clipped across the face, things were looking grim. Kamasawa then appeared and there was quite an argument between him and Four Eyes. In the end it was agreed that we could stay in the hut on condition that, if one of the other parties fell behind in their work, we would turn out and help them so that we could all finish at 5pm. A pack of cards was produced and we settled down to enjoy our afternoon. About 4pm Kamasawa returned and told us that one of the groups unloading the coal wagons was behind. So we put on our coats and turned out to help them. We were all finished by 5pm and from then on we were able to negotiate the workload on the coal wharf – but not on any other job.

Back at camp there was much excitement and the POWs whose work was within the camp told us that a lorry had arrived, filled with cardboard boxes stamped with mark of the Red Cross. We could hardly contain ourselves and the rumours were rife. However it was more than a week before we heard any more about these Red Cross parcels. It was on a yasume day that the hut orderlies were summoned down to the admin offices and came back with word that the Japs intended to dish out the Red Cross parcels later that day. About lunchtime each hut had to send men down to the stores to collect the parcels and there was no shortage of volunteers for that job. They returned carrying the cardboard boxes which were allocated one per man. Receiving my box, I sat down to contemplate all the items packed inside – there were tins of tea, corned beef, spam, salmon, milk powder, cheese, butter, biscuits, sugar, chocolate and cigarettes. It was like an Aladdin's Cave. The parcels had been packed in South Africa so various products were from there. I lit a cigarette and savoured the cool flavour of the tobacco – after smoking "kinchies", a Japanese brand of cigarette, the difference was simply amazing. We cut our chocolate (a half-pound block in each parcel) into small pieces to be rationed as sparingly as possible. Four of us in our room shared each tin of food to make the tins last – we each ate our share mixed with our rice rations. Some men made gluttons of themselves and ate the contents of their parcels in no time at all. We were all aware that there were more Red Cross parcels in the stores but we also knew that the Japs were having their share of these, even though the parcels were intended for us POWs. Unfortunately there was nothing we could do about it. The guards were quite open about taking these supplies and boasted about the fine food they were eating at our expense. Judging by the number of cigarettes smoked and chocolate consumed, they must have had about four parcels each. We started the ritual of having tea before turning in at night and we enjoyed sitting around with our tin mugs of tea, complete with milk and sugar, and smoking one of our cigarettes. The cigarettes were usually cut into three pieces to make them last longer, these were smoked in a holder. All in all, it was the nearest we could get to paradise in a Japanese POW camp.

We returned to work after our yasume day and back we went to the coal wharf. In the party unloading wagons there were two POWs who had been working for some time with two Japanese girls and had got to know them quite well. Most of us were more interested in food than sex and the subject was not generally discussed – perhaps it was the poor diet that took away any thoughts we might have had. However these two men, perhaps fortified by the good food from the Red Cross parcels, had been telling the girls about the super chocolate they had received from home and had promised to bring some chocolate the next day, to exchange for "favours" from the two girls. Next day we were again at the coal wharf and the two were working with their female companions. The exchange was to be one piece of chocolate for what was on offer but our two eventually decided that their chocolate was preferable and ate it themselves – possibly because the unflattering way that the girls dressed in baggy pants etc was a bit of a turn-off, even though they were actually quite good looking. Anyway the girls were angry and, grabbing their shovels, they chased our two men down the railway line. Our guard that day, Billy Bennett, saw them haring off chased by the two girls and set off in pursuit with his rifle and bayonet. He was furious that they had been away from work but, when he heard the tale, he saw the funny side and they received only a slap across the face. We were working elsewhere on the wharf when all this happened but heard the full story when we all stopped for lunch.

We were again sent to the ice cold store but this time, instead of working outside the building, our group was detailed to work inside with a group of Japanese stevedores. Our job was to collect boxes of fish from the lift, then carry these to specific storage rooms and stack them. It was freezing cold working here all day but there were compensations. Firstly, we had neither guards nor hanchos with us – it was too cold for them to hang around. Secondly, we could chew raw fish all day long without any risk of beatings. In one of the storage rooms, a Japanese stevedore broke open a wooden box and gave each of us a piece of fish shaped like a large coin. It tasted very good and, as the box was left open, we just helped ourselves until everything had been eaten. We later discovered that we had been eating frozen oysters – no wonder they tasted so good. When we stopped for lunch the Japanese workers allowed us to sit in their hut and, when they saw our poor rations, they collected some fish and made a superb soup, one of my tastiest meals for a very long time. Before we resumed work, one of these stevedores took a large box of fish and demonstrated his lifting technique. Squatting cross-legged in front of a box that he had stood on its end, he placed his shoulder against the box and, with his two lifting hooks, pulled the box on to his shoulder. Finally, with a grunt, he heaved himself to his feet. This was no mean feat and, of course, he turned to us and asked if we could match it. These workers loved to show off their strength and were extremely fit and strong as their job consisted of doing nothing but carrying these heavy loads. Perhaps foolishly, we decided to accept the challenge and Joe stepped forward.

In his first attempt the heavy box pulled him backwards but, after dropping the box a couple of times, he finally mastered the technique. The others in our group followed and eventually all ten of us could perform this lift. The Japs congratulated us and, for the rest of the day, they kept us supplied with cigarettes. We had proved that we were as good as they were. However they could never understand why we had not chosen to kill ourselves rather than be captured as prisoners of war.

Old dockside building in Hakodate – possibly the ice cold store where POWs carried crates of fish they had unloaded from fishing vessels
Photo: Nigel Brown 1997

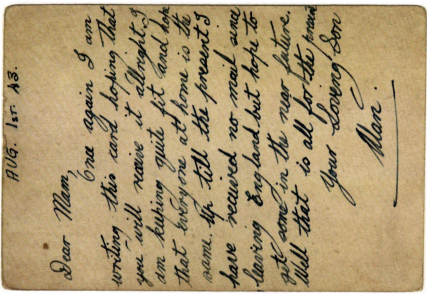

Postcards sent by Alan in 1943/1944 show that he was becoming increasingly concerned that he had received no news from home. He was unaware that incoming mail for the POWs at Hakodate was being deliberately impounded and would not be released until Spring 1944.

CHAPTER THIRTEEN

AUTUMN AND WINTER 1943

The summer of 1943 had faded and we were getting well into autumn – the weather had changed and the glorious warm days were now a thing of the past. Rain and winds became the normal pattern and we realised that another winter would soon be upon us. Even though the summer weather had been so good, the death rate in the camp had slowed down only slightly and the sad processions of dead friends up the hill to the crematorium reminded us that the coming winter would reduce our chances of survival, unless we could steer clear of dysentery and other infections. Our food did not help as the rations of rice contained weevils and maggots too numerous to be removed before cooking. The cry would go up from the food orderlies that there was "meat in the rice" and generally we would eat everything. We also ate bones from any fish we had stolen and cooked, and horse bones that the cookhouse had used for stock for the soup – they had been boiled for so long that they were soft and easy to chew.

About this time we were working on the fish quay and our job was to carry and stack boxes of whole fresh salmon. The fish were packed in salt in these wooden boxes by Japanese women who would reject any fish that had gone off. We could take chunks of these discarded fish as long as we were not caught by the guards or hanchos. We found that the best to eat were the ones we called the "cheesiest" – although these fish were starting to go bad they still tasted good to us. We carried the boxes into the warehouse and, under the supervision of two Japanese stevedores, stacked them. We were able to keep some salmon by concealing it in a mound of rock salt on the quayside then, on the last trip before lunch, we gave a piece to each of our pals to hide in their bento boxes, under the rice. We had to be careful as Four Eyes kept snooping around while we were working. We continued work in the afternoon and, whilst lifting the boxes, I decided that I would try to smuggle a whole fish back to the camp that evening. When work was nearly finished I selected a salmon, making sure it was about the same length as my leg. I then made an excuse to go to the benjo and there I tied the tail of the salmon to a rope which went around my waist under my shirt, the salmon going down the leg of my trousers. Marching back to camp was an unpleasant experience, the salmon flapping against my leg and its salt coating starting to irritate my upper thigh. By the time I reached the camp gates I was walking like an old man, with the pouring rain making things worse, washing the salt into all sorts of places! The rain was actually a blessing as the guards were also soaked and wanted to get into the guardhouse as soon as possible rather than taking time to search us thoroughly. Once in the hut, I concealed the fish under my blankets while I made off to the bathhouse. On the way back I called into the cookhouse and, after promising one of the cooks a piece of the salmon in exchange for a bucket of boiling water, returned to the hut and chopped the fish into cutlets. One of these was kept for the cook and the rest were dropped into the bucket of water and covered with a towel. By the time our rice ration had arrived and was dished out, the salmon cutlets were cooked and we had them with our rice. The eight of us in our room all agreed that it was the best meal we had eaten since the days of the Red Cross parcel. Although it took almost a week for the salt rash on my legs to clear up, I decided that if I had the chance again I would take another salmon.

On one of the days at the coal wharf we had worked all morning loading baskets of coal but the ship's plimsoll line remained resolutely above the water. Although we had loaded more than the required number of baskets, loading at least 100 tons in total, the captain insisted that his ship had not been fully loaded and that our baskets must have been underweight. After some discussion, Hammer Chops the hancho agreed that we must carry on with our work. After lunch we continued loading and our baskets were heaped up with around 50 kg of coal. This was over the normal weight and we couldn't understand why the damned ship was still showing the plimsoll line. By about 4pm we and Hammer Chops were totally fed up and he told the captain that we had loaded more than enough and he was getting no more – we reckoned we had loaded around 200 tons, twice the normal amount. The crew trimmed the coal to level it off and started the engine to pull away from the quay. There was a terrible grating noise and this got worse. The problem was that the ship was grounded. The captain's requests for us to unload some coal were met with a hostile response from Hammer Chops and, when our launches left to take us back, we could see the ship's crew working their guts out, trying to unload enough coal to get the ship afloat!

It was now November going into December and we had been POWs for 20 months. Since leaving Java to "go to a better climate" we had seen the deaths of many in our party. A group of Americans had by now arrived at the camp, having been captured at sea by a German raider. Some of them had been badly wounded but doctors on board the German ship had been very efficient and had saved their lives. One of the Americans had a broad scar like a belt around his waist – this was where he had been operated on after having his stomach shot away by machine gun fire. The Germans had landed the survivors in Tokyo after keeping them on board their ship for six weeks – they had apologised to the Americans for having to hand them over to the Japs.

We saw our first snow, heralding the start of winter, while we were working out in the bay loading a ship with boxes of tinned salmon. The snow fell gently at first but was very heavy by lunchtime with the wind whipping it up into a blizzard. The sling we had loaded on the barge disappeared into the snow as it was hauled up. It was quite dangerous working in these conditions because the Japs operating the cranes and their colleagues giving them signals could not see the slings or each other. Therefore there were many mishaps as loads caught the ship's rail, tipping the boxes on to the barge and its POW workers. We recognised the risks and, when a full sling was hoisted up to the ship, we scattered to the far end of the barge until the empty sling was returned. In such blizzards we could open some tins and eat the fish without anyone seeing us – we took full advantage of this. We were hauled up to the ship, hanging from the last load, and looking like snowmen. Waiting for another barge to arrive, we sat in the hold to keep dry. The weather was so atrocious that the other barge never arrived and, as we were nearing our time to return to shore, our launch was summoned. It took over half an hour to arrive and we piled in to the open well. The journey was a nightmare as visibility was nil and, as the shore was about ¼ mile away and couldn't be seen, we got lost two or three times and nearly rammed ships lying at anchor in the bay. We finally arrived at a jetty which was not our intended destination so had to march the rest of the way to join the POWs who had been working elsewhere.

Some of us who had been working on the barge had concealed tins of salmon and were taking a chance that the bad weather would dissuade the guards from mounting a full search. When we reached camp we were immediately dismissed to our huts. The eight of us in our room had brought back 24 tins in total and we tucked these away in our secret store, hidden above the ceiling. All we needed to do was remove the strips of beading which joined the square plywood panels and push our spoils up there. Replacing the panel and beading did not take very long – it was the perfect place for most things to be hidden. There was only one drawback, the rats that roamed the roof void above us – this was their domain and they ate everything they could so some things had to be concealed elsewhere. Rats were a nuisance generally in the camp and fouled the rice which was in hessian sacks in the camp storehouse. We also had a big problem with the fleas that came with the rats – our blankets and the "tatami" mattresses were infested with these fleas and they used to make meals of us every night whilst we were sleeping. At night the rats would run around in the roof space above us and, as they ran over the plywood ceiling panels, we would be showered with fleas. Our biggest worry was typhus – fortunately none of us caught this terrible scourge.

With the cold weather and snow arriving, the huts we lived in were as cold as the ice store where we worked. Consequently we started to wear all the clothes we possessed in an effort to keep warm. There was nowhere to dry anything that we washed so our clothing became quite dirty and attracted lice. About this time the camp was also hit by a plague of scabies and most of us had sores between our fingers and also our toes. The itching was terrible and, as there was no medication in the camp to relieve this, we were kept awake at night. This, combined with the flea bites, made life unbearable at times.

We looked forward to our yasume day which arrived about every three weeks. Then we would laze around and chat about home. There were card games in some of the huts and, when playing poker, the stakes were sometimes very high as they were playing for rice rations – I saw some men lose a week's rations in one game. This was OK if you were working at the docks as there was always an opportunity to steal food but if you were confined to camp either by being sick or being a camp worker, then you would have to be a fool to join in these card games. Not all the games were for such high stakes – the bridge and whist schools used to go on all day. We also used yasume days to catch up on chores and would pull our room to pieces, shaking out the blankets, mats and any spare clothing to get rid of the fleas. Haircuts were usually in demand and the barbers (anyone who could wield a pair of scissors) charged for their efforts in cigarettes. During the winter we kept our hair to repel the cold and the only time we had it cut was when the Japs ordered us. The guards still patrolled the huts during yasume, generally making a nuisance of themselves – we had to salute (or bow to them if not wearing a hat).

Hat wearing was a difficult area as it was not obvious exactly when you were regarded as being inside or outside a hut. We had a guard who slapped us around for wearing our caps when inside, but he also did the same for not wearing our caps when outside. He used to stand at the door leading from the corridor out to the courtyard and, if you put your cap on before going through the doorway, he would slap you around the head. If however you went through the doorway and then put your cap on, you were hit for being outside without a hat. To counter this, we would try to get as many people through the door as possible, in groups.

There had been a distribution of the balance of Red Cross parcels that were left in the stores and this worked out at one parcel for every six men. Two of the eight POWs in our room were away in the camp's hospital so we had an entire parcel to divide amongst the six of us. At first this seemed to be an impossible task but we decided to open only one tin at a time and share the contents to supplement our rice rations. So the parcel lasted us quite some time. On Christmas Day however we had a good feed and the Red Cross items, together with some tins of the salmon we had hidden in the ceiling, made it a day to remember. Also the Japs had declared it a yasume day so we lazed around and, in the afternoon, called into the hospital hut to see our two friends who were sick with dysentery. We found that they would be returning to our room in the near future – their stools were being monitored and they were slowly getting back to normal.

The rats had been overrunning the camp for some time and, due to sacks of rice in the stores being ruined, our rations were cut. On one of our yasume days we sought permission from the Japs to have a rat hunt. Now the Japs were terrified of rats because of the plague that they carried but, as they were now endangering our meagre rations, our only thought was to eliminate them. Having carried most of the sacks of rice to another store room, we could see the holes where the rats were coming and going. We blocked these off with chocks of wood and, after tying up our trousers at the ankles and our coats at the wrists, we armed ourselves with sticks and went into the store room. The door was closed behind us and we proceeded to move the few remaining sacks one at a time, piling them up against the walls. The rats inside and under the sacks ran in all directions and tried to hide in the holes that we had blocked. After ten minutes we had cleared the room of rats and had also knocked the stuffing out of Joe's sandshoes which he had lost whilst kicking out at a rat – we had seen this "rat" flying through the air and beat the living daylights out of it! When we were sure that no rats were still alive, we knocked on the door and were allowed out carrying all that we had killed. The dead rats were laid out on the ground and the Japs were well satisfied, informing us that we could make rat hunting a regular yasume occasion. It had been a change from the ordinary routine of the camp and I think this was the only time that we were in a food store without trying to steal something!

Returning to work at the cold store, our job this time was to load a small coaster with boxes of fish from the store. The winter weather had by now settled into a pattern of snowstorms every day and those of us working inside the cold store were in the best place. The rest of the working party, carrying the boxes across the road and stacking them on to the nets that would be hoisted on to the ship, were cold and wet. To make matters worse, our guard for the day was our old friend Billy Bennett. He wandered around, both inside and outside the store, looking for trouble. By lunchtime he had slapped and kicked most of the men who were working outside on the dock. Those of us inside the store had been quite fortunate for we had escaped without punishment for the whole morning. The Japanese stevedores made a steaming hot fish soup in their yasume hut and we were allowed in there due to the bad weather. They shared this out and each of us got a large mug full of the gorgeous soup. There was a variety of fish in it – white fish which was probably cod, some squid cut into strips, chopped octopus and seaweed. We wolfed this down and were even allowed second helpings as the Japs had only to go outside to collect more ingredients to keep the pot boiling. With food like that, it was no wonder the stevedores were sturdy little men. They also shared cigarettes with us and were amazed when one of the Yanks, a chap from Texas, tore his cigarette to pieces and put the tobacco in his mouth to chew. They said if he wanted tobacco he could take some from a pouch they produced. "Tex" took a big pinch and chewed on it for a while before spitting out the accumulated saliva into an ashcan that was in the corner of the hut. His aim was deadly accurate although he was about ten yards away from the ashcan. The Japs were impressed with his spitting but they could not understand actually chewing tobacco. Tex persuaded two of them to try it with one of them spitting it out immediately and the other chewing once or twice but then swallowing the liquid – he dashed outside and was sick. When he returned he told Tex that it was "dami dami". Nevertheless Tex was showered with tobacco to chew for the rest of the day and the Japs kept bringing others to watch Tex and see him spit out the tobacco juice.

Returning from work that evening in deep snow, we knew that we would have problems getting out of camp next day. However we were not prepared for the sight that greeted us next morning for, as we opened the door to get out to the cookhouse to collect our rations, we were amazed to find the entire doorway completely blocked with snow. Using pieces of wood we dug ourselves out and cleared a path to the cookhouse. We paraded in the snow and the numbers declared sick were greater than usual as no one fancied turning out to march to work. The Jap medical orderly made short work of the sick parade and reported that virtually everyone was fit to work. So, off to work we marched, wrapped in as many clothes as we could find. Fortunately the snow was like powder and did not make us wet. The wind was icy and cut right through our clothing and into our bones. By the time we had broken through the snow drifts on the way down the hill to the town, we were all sweating with sheer exertion.

Our job that day was on the coal wharf and, with the savage wind that day, our boats across the bay were buffeted about in the waves. We had to pump the water out with two hand pumps and were frozen stiff by the time we eventually arrived at the coal wharf, having had to seek safer waters by taking a longer route skirting around the edge of the bay. The Jap hanchos who all worked for the Kairak company were not happy about our arriving late as they had to move a set amount of coal in the day. We set to work but found that the wet coal had frozen solid inside the wagons – the trap doors used for dropping the coal had also frozen. The only way we could shift the coal was to get in the wagon and dig it out. We were issued with straw-platted gloves to protect our hands from the metal parts of the shovels which were so cold they would have given us frost-burns on our hands. Lunch was taken late as we needed to clear all the wagons beforehand, it was also shorter than normal, just 30 minutes. After lunch we cleared the coal using the familiar baskets supported on poles, carrying these to the other side of the wharf. It took us all afternoon to clear the coal and, as the snow had continued all day, the launches never turned up to take us back across the bay. That meant an additional march of six or seven miles around the bay to get us back to the town jetty before the usual march back to camp – in blizzard conditions. By the time we arrived back, we were so exhausted that we could barely eat our rice.

The next day we were again at the coal wharf but our job this time was to clear a pile of coal from a former quarry, where the coal had built up over a period of time, to the dockside. On this occasion we were not loading on to any ship as very few such vessels were coming to collect coal - the severe weather had presumably confined them to their home ports. We started work on the frozen coal which was in a mound about 15 feet high. Loosening the coal was hard work and we had to use picks before we could make any impression on it. It was then shovelled into baskets and carried in the usual way to the wharf. As we loosened and dug away at the base of the pile, we had created an overhang that was too high to reach. We expected this would fall into the hole we had created. Stopping for lunch in the yasume hut, we got a roaring fire going and were happily drying out after the morning blizzards, generating a great deal of steam from our wet clothing. The guards had to kick us and use their rifle butts to get us back to work. After we resumed digging there was a cracking noise and the overhang collapsed, scattering coal everywhere. We dived out of the way but some of the coal, frozen in larger lumps, gave a few of us some nasty bruises. One of our diggers, a chap called Tiny, tripped over an abandoned shovel and was trapped by a huge piece of frozen coal – this had trapped one of his legs, from the knee down. We hurriedly cleared the coal away so that he could get out. We then took him to the yasume hut where the guards and hancho found that his leg was broken below the knee, on the front of his shin. It was decided that he would have to be carried back to the camp but of course there was no transport back across the bay until the end of the afternoon. Tiny was in considerable pain so we made a splint and lashed his two feet together to keep the broken leg stiff. We made a stretcher from spars of wood and six of us shouldered the weight and started off for camp – some 10 miles away. There were twelve of us in total so we would be able to share the work of carrying him back. Tiny was a six-footer and, although he had lost weight during his time as a POW, he was still quite heavy to carry. The snow drifts were an obstacle and, as we struggled, Yah Yah the guard kept shouting "speedo". We soon got fed up with him and told him to either help us carry Tiny or shut up, all expressed in an explosion of earthy language! We finally staggered into the camp and took Tiny straight to the hut used as a hospital. The Jap medical orderly called out the Japanese army doctor whilst we brought in an American naval surgeon. Tiny's leg was in a bad state and the normal procedure would be to amputate but, in civilian life, Tiny was a steeplejack and had to climb for a living. The American surgeon persuaded the Japs to allow him to operate on the leg, first removing all the splintered bones, then shaving the shin bone in Tiny's good leg so that this could be grafted on to the broken shin. He saved the leg and, after a few months, Tiny could walk again with only a hint of a limp. He had to take it easy for some time and had scars on both legs but was only too thankful that he could walk again. Others were not so fortunate for any scratch could turn septic. One man got a fish bone stuck in his throat and, as he couldn't bear to eat with the pain of a septic throat, he eventually died.

Hakodate POW camp huts – these would have been on the land shown on pages 70 & 76 – the site was cleared some years ago. The lower slopes of Mount Hakodate can be seen in the background. The caption 函館捕広収容所 translates as Hakodate internment or labour camp.

Photo from a Hakodate local history journal, probably taken shortly after the war

CHAPTER FOURTEEN

ILLNESS & DISEASE

The intense cold caused the water to freeze, meaning that running water was a luxury we could enjoy only in the summer. Working conditions began to take their toll and our wet clothing would often be frozen solid by next morning. It had to thaw out while we were wearing it, meaning that we all suffered from aches and pains. Footwear was also a concern – most of us were wearing clogs with wooden soles that only roughly matched the shape of our feet. The uppers were from our old boots, attached to the soles by wire strapping wrapped around and nailed in place. This technique made good solid laced-up clogs! The problem was that the snow tended to stick to the bottom of the clogs, making them very dangerous to wear when loading ships with coal, increasing the chances of falling off the planks into the water (or into the hold).

As winter wore on, frostbite was affecting some men but they had great difficulty persuading the Japanese medical orderly that they were having trouble walking. Whenever anyone reported sick, our doctor and his orderlies tried to convince the Japs but they had the last word and sent many to work who later finished up in hospital or died. Frostbite could turn the toes black and gangrenous, resulting in toes being amputated to save the foot. Men who had their big toes amputated could not walk very well as this affected their balance. They could not march to work so spent their days wandering around the camp and being harassed by the guards who would not allow them to light the stoves until the workers arrived back at the end of the day. Their days were long, cold and miserable.

One very wintery morning we paraded for work and, after the usual ritual of being counted and split into work parties, we marched out of the gates. The road outside the camp was high above the bay so we always tried to get an idea of the type of journey we would have on the small boats which took us out across the bay. On this particular morning we saw anchored close inshore a ship flying a flag that we had never seen before. Ships were never anchored in this part of the bay as there was no shelter of any description. We were therefore very interested why it should be there and what the flag was. We worked that day in one of the many warehouses that were scattered around the bay, all with their own jetties where barges could either pull alongside or tie up at the end of the jetty. We had to move bags of salt on to a barge for transporting across the bay to the ice cold store. We had of course previously worked at the cold store unloading salt from barges into the store so we guessed we would probably be sent there next day to unload it all again! We worked all day with only a 30 minute break for lunch – we were cold and hungry as there was no food to steal, only salt.

On our return to camp we had to walk through a disinfectant-filled trough, making sure that our boots were completely soaked with it. We were mystified and questioned the guards about this. They were as dumbfounded as we were and asked their colleagues "nanda?" (why?) - the answer came back that the ship anchored in the bay below the camp had sick men on board and that a group of buildings just outside our camp was being used as an isolation hospital. When questioned further, they told us the disease was typhus and that the sick men were the fishermen for whom we had loaded stores on to their ship, and that this was the ship. On the island where these men spent the fishing season, their huts had been overrun with rats and the fleas had spread the disease. Typhus is contagious and it had spread throughout their close-knit fishing community. Our problem was that we had rats in all of our huts and these were almost certainly also in the huts now being used as an isolation area for the fishermen. Clearly the rats could easily move to and fro between the two camps as they were separated by a space of only 200 yards.

When we turned out for work next morning we had to march past the isolation camp and could see the fishermen walking around in the grounds. Our thought was that there couldn't be much wrong with them if they were able to wander around like that. The ship had discharged all crew, passengers and cargo to the isolation camp and was still flying the unusual flag. No other vessels were coming anywhere near it. When we returned to camp after work we again had to walk through the disinfectant and were also sprayed with it, drenching our clothes. We were all glad to have a good long soak in the bathhouse. The men who had been in the camp all day told us that funeral vans had been running from the isolation camp up the hill to the crematorium all day long. We could only pray that the disease would not get into our camp. The Japanese staff and guards were probably more scared than we were for the next day we were all given an injection. We were on tenterhooks when anyone in our camp came out in a rash as this can be one of the symptoms of typhus but our red rashes were in fact from the salt we were working with.

When marching to work one morning, about two weeks after the ship had anchored in the bay below us, we noticed that there were two tugs anchored alongside. On their decks were large tanks with hoses going into the contaminated ship. The people handling these hoses were in white boiler suits with special headgear – they were fumigating the ship. When we returned that evening the ship had gone but, in the isolation camp, the lights were burning so we knew there were still inmates. The funeral vans continued for another two weeks and after that we saw the huts being fumigated and realised that the disease had run its course. When we questioned the guards they said we had been very fortunate that the typhus had not spread to our camp and that there had been no survivors in the isolation camp, 100 fishermen having died of the disease.

Life eventually settled down although we continued to have deaths caused by beri-beri and dysentery. The harsh winter had not helped. There was also a new horror to cope with – septicaemia. We were finding that any scratch or sore turned septic due to our poor state of nutrition. About this time I had toothache and, as it grew worse, I had to visit the Jap medical orderly who referred me to a British dentist who was a POW in the camp. He checked me over and told me that I would need a filling in one of the back molars. He set up a contraption made from a bicycle wheel linked by a chain to a gear wheel which, when controlled by a pedal, operated the dentist's drill (made from a sharpened piece of wire). I sat on a stool with my mouth open and turned the pedal which operated the drill. Whenever I felt pain I stopped turning the pedal and the drill stopped immediately. After drilling out the tooth he mixed a filling – God alone knows what ingredients he used – and pressed it into the cavity. My mouth was sore for a few days afterwards but the filling stayed put. In fact I still had this filling when the war finished.

After the injection when typhus was rampant in the isolation camp, the Japs continued to give us injections but did not tell us what they were for. My arm was like a pincushion from all the jabs I received with blunt needles. I think they were probably testing out new serums and drugs on us although I must say that I have not suffered any ill effects from these injections.

CHAPTER FIFTEEN

LIFE IMPROVES (SLIGHTLY)

One day whilst working at the coal wharf, our guard Yah Yah was eating an apple and we commented how we liked apples. When we asked where the apple had come from, he blew up and walked away shouting we were "dami dami" and "bugero". However about half an hour later he came back and called me over. I was expecting a kick or punch as Yah Yah was always very unpredictable but he said that if we had any money he would buy a sack of apples for us and we could eat them in the yasume hut before we left for camp. None must be taken back nor anything said in camp about his buying apples for us. Now the Japs had recently decided in their generosity to pay us for our work at the wonderful rate of 10 sen (about 6d in British money) per day. If you worked for three weeks with only a break on yasume day, you accumulated 2 yen. By selling us small macaroon biscuits at 5 sen each they made a fantastic profit on their biscuits. Yah Yah's offer to buy a sack of apples for 5 yen was much better value so the ten of us decided to stump up 50 sen each and gave the money to Yah Yah.

We worked solidly until lunchtime and trooped into the yasume hut looking forward to having at least one or two apples with our lunch. Yah Yah was sitting in front of the stove which was well alight and, as we could not see our sack of apples, we thought we had been taken for a ride. After waiting until we were all there and checking outside to make sure there were no kempeitai in sight, he went into a corner and pulled out a straw sack that was hidden under some matting. In the manner of a magician, he pulled out one of the most gorgeous apples we had ever seen – the plump luscious fruit looked too good to eat. The skin was a golden yellow with a bright red patch on one side. Yah Yah passed the apple to Joe who was sitting beside him and he passed it around the group of us, sitting in a circle around the stove. Yah Yah dug into the sack again and brought out more apples, all as tempting as the first, and soon all of us were munching away. He said we could each have one more apple and that he would take the balance back to camp for his colleagues.

Whilst Yah Yah had been handing out the apples, Joe had been undoing the stitching on the side of the sack and had made a hole large enough to get his hand in. As we argued about the number of apples we were getting, Joe was busy taking fruit out of the hole and surreptitiously passing it around. Before Yah Yah proceeded to delve for each man's second apple, we had succeeded in acquiring about four illicit apples each. Joe still had his hand in the sack and Yah Yah, delving into the sack, found Joe's fingers. We waited in trepidation for the explosion of temper but, as Joe swiftly removed his hand, Yah Yah threw the sack up in the air and ran out of the hut screaming that there was a rat in the sack. Of course we grabbed some of the apples and hid them in our clothing then, while some of us were hammering the wooden floor to make it sound like we were chasing the rat, the others replaced the rest of the apples in the sack, but only after removing a small bite-sized chunk from some of them. When Yah Yah came back we said the rat had escaped and gave him the sack so that he could give us our "second" apple. He wasn't keen to put his hand back in the sack so Joe and I pulled out some apples and showed him the damage where they looked to have been nibbled by the rat. He said we could have the whole sack and wandered out in a less than happy mood. We had to eat all the apples before we returned to camp!

Felix the camp commandant decided one day that we should all learn to sing Japanese marching songs. We would then be able to march to work singing, like the Japs. Two songs were taught and, as anyone not singing received a beating, we soon learned both tune and words. We had no idea what the words meant but Felix was quite happy when we marched out singing. We added a few of our own phrases which, to say the least, were not very complimentary.

In the years that we were prisoners some men never managed to learn any of the Japanese language. Others, such as those of us working each day with Japanese people, did pick up a good amount, enough for example to be able to make basic conversation with the stevedores. There were two POWs in the camp who worked so hard on the language that they could read the occasional newspaper that we picked up while out at work. These newspapers were full of anti-American propaganda which we reckoned was to keep up morale as the local food situation, other than fish, was poor.

We were looking forward to warmer days after the harsh winter. There had been some deaths caused by men just losing the will to live – no amount of coaxing could bring them out of the deep depression that set in. They simply laid down and died.

Having told the Japs for a long time that we would rather have bread for our meals instead of rice, one morning they singled out three men to build a bread oven. The POWs were agog with excitement about having our own bakehouse however this was to take another month or so as the oven had to be made and assembled first. The great day eventually arrived and one of the cooks, who was an armourer in the RAF and hadn't cooked anything until he was taken prisoner by the Japs, was delegated as baker. The oven was fired with wood, the flour and yeast drawn from the stores and the dough mixed. After rising it had to be rationed into approximately 200 pieces all the same size, then rolled out by hand into small rounds about 6" in diameter. After baking they were put on trays to cool and were ready for our evening meal. The oven proved temperamental and that first baking was not a success – the bread cakes had not cooked properly and were stodgy and yeasty. We ate them with our watery soup but found that we were still hungry – they were not as filling as our usual ration of rice. A batch had also been baked for the Jap guards and they were so disgusted with the end product that they dumped their bread cakes in the pig bin (these were later retrieved and shared out by the POWs). We reverted to rice rations whilst the baker tried to master the vagaries of the oven. Then a week later, after various small batches had been tested, another 200 bread cakes were made and rationed out with the soup. This time the baking was perfect and the bread tasted superb. As usual there was not enough of it and we went to bed very hungry. After that, bread was on the menu at least once a week and in our room we tried to steal tinned or salted salmon to accompany our bread.

We had by now established an area of land for gardening and we grew pumpkins, potatoes and daikon for use in the cookhouse, the pumpkins being used to thicken up the soups which we had every day. The men who stayed in the camp each day tended the garden, helped by the walking sick. The "no work, no eat" rule imposed by the Japs meant that the cookhouse was issued with only enough rations to feed the men who were working. Our toilets in the camp, which were removable metal containers under a hole in the floor, had to be emptied frequently. This involved two men carrying the heavy metal container on a bamboo pole and, with our garden now an important source of food, we saw this as an opportunity to help our plants grow. The contents were simply emptied on to the soil around the plants – perhaps not the most hygienic practice but it certainly made the plants grow.

Carrying the toilet container could be a hazardous job, especially when one man was much taller than the other. When I was first detailed for the task, I was with a chap much taller than my 5 ft 8 in. The container kept sliding along the bamboo pole towards me and carrying it down the steps resulted in my being showered with excrement that was slopping over the top. On that occasion I had been at the front so next time I had to "carry the can" I chose to be at the rear of the pole. The damned contained swung back and forth and, as it slid towards me, I dared not shout out as there was a risk I would get a mouthful of our load. I resorted to pushing back the container with my hand but still got soaked up my sleeve, on my face and down the front of my coat. I was in a terrible state by the time we had emptied the containers from all of the huts – so malodorous that the Japs at the guardroom did not want me to stop and salute them. It was strange how the Japs would choose two men of unequal height for this task – I swear that the sadistic little sods did it deliberately. After a bath to get rid of the filth I then had to wash all the clothes I had been wearing, and this without any soap!

On one occasion we were working in a warehouse close to the naval dockyard where we had first started our work in December 1942. Our job was to move boxes of tinned crayfish on to a barge. Kamasawa was our hancho and Billy Bennett our guard. We seized an opportunity when both were away in the office to sample the contents of the tins. A box was broken open and we needed to dispose of its 48 tins of crayfish before the Japs came back from the office. Since the delivery of the Red Cross parcels we now came to work properly equipped, for in every parcel was a small folding tin opener which could be concealed between two fingers when being searched. A tin could now be opened and its contents devoured in no time at all. This is what we did and, between ten of us, the delicious crayfish disappeared in minutes, the empty tins being dumped behind a large stack of boxes in a corner of the warehouse. We were so full that we had to take our lunchtime rice rations back to camp.

On a visit to the toilet that day (the traditional benjo, cantilevered on two beams stretching over the wharf), I was confronted by a sight that I shall never forget. Literally hundreds of Chinese prisoners were being used to dig out a new dry dock, and to carry away the earth. They reminded me of a line of ants, there were so many of them. Overseeing them were Japanese army guards, each equipped with a long leather bullwhip, and the luckless Chinese workers were being constantly flayed with these whips. I had not realised that there were such prisoners in Hakodate but clearly the Chinese were being used for the type of manual work that would have killed us off very quickly – nothing mechanical was being used, just sheer manpower. The deeper the Chinese dug, the harder it must have been to carry out the earth in their baskets and a naval dry dock is very deep indeed.

We had discussed various ways of doing away with the horrible chore of toilet emptying and eventually the idea of a cesspit at the lowest point in the camp was the decision. This called for a new block of toilets to be built with drainage pipes and a system of flushing so that everything drained down to the pit. Plans were drawn up and presented to the Japs who were immediately interested in the idea. 20 of the fittest men were withdrawn from outside work to dig the cesspit. Our gang of 10 was part of this workforce. We marked out an area approximately 15 feet by 20 feet and started digging. The soil was taken in handcarts which we constructed, out of the main gates and was tipped down the hillside towards the bay. It took about a week to dig out the hole to a depth of about 10 feet. Then a central baffle had to be made in concrete so a template of shuttering was used, balanced on small concrete posts positioned in the centre of the pit. We mixed concrete with sand, stones and cement which the Japs provided and filled the central barrier with it. During our work we had a steady stream of visitors as the Japs had never seen anything like this in Hokkaido – they asked all manner of questions and our engineers had their work cut out trying to explain how the cesspit would work. Meanwhile a team of joiners was busy constructing a new toilet block with wooden seating laid over downpipes linked to a central drain which had a good fall to the cesspit. The engineers had to devise a scheme to convert an ordinary tap to provide enough pressure to flush the drain. After much experimentation they came up with a large scoop made of wood but lined with tin which resembled a small wheelbarrow without the wheels. This was balanced under a water tap which was left running very slowly. The scoop was on a pivot and, as it filled up, the front end became so heavy that it tilted and emptied its contents (about 2 gallons) down the pipe immediately below it. This volume of water flowing through the pipes at intervals of 5-10 minutes, day and night, would keep the drains clear.

By this time we had finished the cesspit, complete with an outflow pipe close to the top (on the opposite side to the pipe that would introduce the foul water) and a cover made from wooden planks. To start the bacteria that was needed to run the cesspit, we caught and killed a few rats and threw them in. We were ready to start the system and Felix the camp commandant brought in some of his army friends for the occasion. With the whole camp assembled on a yasume day, the water tap was turned on by Felix. We knew that the scoop would take a long time to fill so we turned the tap on full. Having watched the scoop tilt and drop its water into the pipe, the Japs scuttled down the corridor, following the water down to the new toilets. After this, they hurried down to the cesspit to see the first lot of water arrive in the cesspit. There was much fascination and, for the rest of the day, we had Japs including the guards and office staff running up and down the corridors, in and out of the new toilets, and peering down the cesspit. No one could use the toilets that day as there was no privacy, especially as the Japanese girls from the office were also popping in to see the system flushing.

It took about a week for the cesspit to fill up. As predicted by our engineers, the water from the outflow pipe was clean – this was channelled to a tank and used for watering the gardens. The old toilets were now closed off and everyone had to use the new facilities. Our days of toilet emptying had ended and not before time! The only loss was to the garden for, without the sludge, the plants took longer to grow. Existing on camp rations without any opportunity to supplement these with stolen food was a hardship. The only extra food during our period of digging came from Felix although he didn't know it. He had a dog which wandered into our excavations. It was killed, skinned and cooked before he knew it was missing. We shared the meat which, although slightly stringy, tasted like mutton. Perhaps Felix suspected what had happened to the dog but he couldn't prove anything. He did not replace the dog.

A new parade ground was required and, after seeing our work digging the cesspit, Felix gave instructions to us to dig out part of the sloping hillside in the middle of the camp. We worked on this for two weeks and had to build a dry-stone retaining wall. The earth was again to be dumped down the slope leading to the water's edge. Ferrying this excess earth out of the camp, we had to pass the admin buildings and of course the guardroom. Those of us pushing the handcart had to stop every time we passed the guardhouse and salute the guard who was sitting in a chair enjoying the sunny weather. Over the other side of the road, on a square in front of the admin buildings, Felix was putting the rest of the guards through a course of bayonet practice – for this they used wooden rifles with leather pads on the tips. He was also practising with a wooden sword, pitching himself against the guards with their imitation rifles. We stopped and watched this for a while then carried on with our work.

Each time we passed this drill practice we took the opportunity to stop and rest. Felix saw us and enquired whether I would like to try my hand with one of the wooden guns. I declined, telling him that I was an airman and not accustomed to handling a rifle and bayonet so he asked the others whether they would like to have a go. He was so insistent that eventually an Indonesian corporal from the Dutch army said he would, expecting his opponent to be one of the guards. However Felix picked up a rifle himself and then the fun started for our champion was well versed in the art of self-defence. Felix made two or three lunges which were parried with no difficulty, then he became more and more frustrated as he couldn't break down the resistance of our corporal. His actions turned more violent and wild then, as he came forward, our corporal used his rifle to guide Felix's weapon harmlessly over his head and, bringing the butt end of his rifle around quickly, it clipped the side of Felix's unprotected jaw. A look of amazement spread across the face of the commandant and we stood petrified, waiting for the explosion of wrath whilst two guards grabbed the corporal and disarmed him. Felix stood there like a statue then, rubbing his jaw, he stormed at the guards who were holding the corporal and told them to release him. Then, walking across to him, he picked up one of imitation rifles and we all thought this was the end for our Indonesian friend. But no, he asked him to demonstrate how he had managed to hit him across the jaw. After a few minutes Felix was quite proficient at this and dismissed us. We went back to the rest of our group who were still digging and related the story – having been away so long, they had imagined we were detained at the guardhouse for some misdemeanour.

After lunch we were again on our trek with the handcart and, passing the square, we saw that all the guards were there and Felix was showing off his newly acquired skills. We also noticed that the guards were nursing their jaws as Felix had been knocking hell out of them using the technique he had learned that morning. He gave a broad grin as we passed by, it made him look even more like the well-fed cat that had inspired his nickname. We completed the new parade ground and would now be able to return to outside work, a welcome prospect after several weeks existing on camp rations. However our first day was to be at the coal wharf and, after boarding the launches to take us across the bay, I was aware that the buildings seemed to be moving. At first I thought that it was the wash from the ferry that was passing by. Yah Yah our guard said it was likely to be an earth disturbance caused by one of Hokkaido's volcanoes – an earthquake! The peaks of the mountainous area surrounding the town of Hakodate were a familiar scene but this was still a frightening experience for us. Back at camp that evening we found that the tremor had lasted two or three minutes and had shaken the huts. During the night that followed, we had further tremors and these were more worrying as we were not allowed out of the building which was swaying and groaning under the strain. The roof and beams rattled alarmingly and, if they collapsed, we were in serious danger. Needless to say, there were no guards in the hut that night, they were all outside.

Our smuggled stocks of stolen and black market goods continued to be a life saver. The store up above the ceiling was pretty full when disaster struck. Whilst we were out at work one day, Sgt Saito and the guards made a thorough search of the camp. They were looking for a radio as they knew we were getting outside news from somewhere. One of our camp-based friends told us that the search party apparently noticed the ceiling panel beading was loose and, having poked a bayonet at it, the panel was dislodged. Tins of food and other goods had cascaded from the ceiling. When we arrived at camp that evening, dirty after working on the coal wharf, we were all looking forward to a hot bath but, instead of being dismissed, we were assembled on the parade ground. Felix the commandant arrived and gave us a lecture which was translated by the Jap interpreter. We were not paying any real attention to this until he said that the occupants of Hut 4 had to stay behind. After dismissing the others, we were marched up to our hut and the sight that greeted us was incredible. There, piled up on the floor of our room, was everything that we had stolen and smuggled into camp. It was just like a grocer's shop with tins of salmon and crayfish, packets of tea, soap, cigarettes all on display. We were bundled out and marched down to the guardhouse, beaten and put in the cells. The cells were built of rough pinewood tree trunks and the entrance to each cell was a half-height door that had to be negotiated on hands and knees. There was no evening meal.

Next morning we were given a small rice ball and a cup of hot water for breakfast. We were then called out of the cells by Four Eyes, arguably the worst of the guards who booted us as we crawled out. We were then counted, this being a necessary ritual that the Japs observed, even when it was obvious that no one could have escaped. We were marched to the bathhouse and allowed to wash faces and hands, without soap, and had to dry ourselves on our shirts. We were then marched to the guardroom and put back in our cells. When the day's work parties appeared, we were hauled out of the cells and put at the head of the column. Kamasawa the hancho was told that we were a disgrace and that we should be given no privileges. Work that day was an unrelenting 10 hours, shovelling coal and carrying the heavy baskets. Back at camp that evening, Felix gave us a lecture about stealing from our employers and said that our punishment was 7 days in the cells on reduced rations, with daily work of the heaviest nature that could be found for us.

Those were the longest 7 days that I can remember. We were worked to a standstill every day and the rations of rice were very small. In the cells, until lights out, we were not allowed to sit but were expected to kneel upright on the rough pinewood floor. We were not allowed to ease our aching knees by resting back on our heels. With just one blanket as cushioning, sleep was virtually impossible due to the floor sticking in the ribs. The 7 days eventually passed and we were allowed to return to our hut. We decided that in future we would only steal what could be eaten whilst working. This proved to be a wise move as we were searched thoroughly at the end of every working day. The searches dropped off after a week or so and we did bring back some spoils but tended to eat these immediately or sell anything left over for cigarettes, the main currency in the camp. We no longer stored any of our contraband.

As the war progressed, Japanese forces began to retreat from the islands that they had captured. This started to affect morale and the mood of our guards changed. Some became more violent and took out their frustrations on us. Others, Billy Bennett in particular, were not so stupid and could see that the war was turning against them and that some day soon would come the day of reckoning. He had previously been one of the most vicious Japs I had the misfortune to meet but he was now a changed man. He would bring us sugar and cigarettes and would entreat us to tell the Americans how good he had been to us. Of course we played him along and, when he lost his temper, we would remind him by saying "sensou awari" (what might happen when the war ended!) He would grin and say that he was a good "tomodachi" and that we should tell the Americans this. Little did we realise that it would be another year before we would see that dream fulfilled.

CHAPTER SIXTEEN

A NEW COMMANDANT

After returning from work one day and having our evening meal, Warrant Officer Hattrick was called down to the Japanese officers' quarters. He arrived back about 30 minutes later with news that Felix our camp commandant was being transferred. Next morning Felix himself took the salute and confirmed that would indeed be leaving us that very day. At work that day, all talk was about the change of commandant. Felix had mellowed since our arrival and, although he could be volatile, he was at least someone we knew – better the devil you know…

The camp operated without a commandant for about a week then, when we returned one evening from work, we found all the camp workers and the sick lined up on the parade ground. We joined them and, after about 15 minutes of waiting for something to happen, we watched as the entire staff of officers and civilians from the administration offices appeared and made their way to the parade ground, lining up with us. The guards also assembled and then a small Japanese officer emerged, flanked by Lt Takahashi and another officer. This was our first sight of the new commanding officer. We were called to attention to salute him.

The new commandant proceeded to address us, not in Japanese but in perfect English. He introduced himself as Colonel Emoto and went on to say that he hoped eventually to speak to us all individually after he had settled in. After being dismissed, all we could talk about was Col Emoto and his command of our language. We were hoping that this would our life a little easier. Of course the guards had not understood a word that he had said and they kept asking us questions. This was a refreshing change for we were used to being lectured in Japanese with their interpreter putting his own slant on what was being said.

There had been a delivery of Red Cross clothing which had been lying in the stores for around six months. When this was brought to the attention of the new commandant, he gave orders for the clothing to be distributed immediately. We all received an American army greatcoat, trousers, a cold weather cap with earflaps, boots, socks and gloves.

When we paraded for work the next day we were better dressed than our Japanese guards and, when the hanchos arrived, they were most impressed with our new attire. We wore the new clothing for a couple of weeks but apparently there were complaints from the civilian population of Hakodate that the prisoners were better dressed than any of them, or indeed the Japanese army. As a result, Col Emoto gave orders that we could not wear our new overcoats or trousers for work, they were to be worn only in the camp. We were still allowed to wear our new boots and hat.

Returning from work one evening, we found great excitement in the camp. The British warrant officer who was used by the Japs as a go-between had been in the administration office and had seen a stack of letters from home that had been censored and were ready for distribution. He had asked one of the officers Lt Takahashi (who spoke quite good English) whether these letters were going to be distributed and had been told they would be handed out on the next yasume day. We could hardly contain ourselves, waiting for the next rest day to arrive. As the Japs did not usually inform us of a yasume day until the day before, we were not sure exactly when this would be. However the long-awaited day duly arrived and, after breakfast had been dished out, the call came on the tannoy for Warrant Officer Hattrick to go to the office. He returned with two sacks of mail and, as the names were called out, we all received one or more letters. The letters had been in the administration offices for many months, supposedly delayed while they awaited the work of the censor.

It was now Spring 1944 and this was the first mail I had seen since leaving home in December 1941. I received six letters from my mother and father, together with a photograph of my two sisters. All was well at home and I now knew they had received the cards that I had been sending for the past year telling them I was alive. The atmosphere in the camp was one of great joy and tranquillity as the men sat reading the news from home. The letters were read over and over again in any spare moments that we had – they seemed to form a bond spanning the thousands of miles between Japan and home.

However not all the letters were as welcome as mine. Some of the lads received news from home of illness and deaths. I remember one chap blowing his top when he read a letter from his fiancée – she had been

TEL: HOLBORN 3434
Extn. 3003.

Any communications on the
subject of this letter
should be addressed to:
　　THE
UNDER SECRETARY OF STATE,
　AIR MINISTRY,
and the following number
quoted:- P.368705/42

AIR MINISTRY,

LONDON, W.C.2.

22nd April 1943.

Sir,
~~Madam,~~

 I am directed to confirm a telegram from this department in which you were notified that information has now been received through the International Red Cross Committee, stating that your Son No. 1125504 Aircraftman First-Class Alan CARTER Royal Air Force, is a prisoner of war.

 The Committee's report quotes Japanese information and states that he is at Hakodate Camp, N. Japan. He should now be able to communicate with you.

 A pamphlet regarding communications with prisoners of war is enclosed as it may be of service to you.

     (Sir,
I am; (~~Madam~~,
    Your obedient Servant,
     J. G. Shreeve
   for Director of Personal Services.

This was sent to Alan's parents in April 1943 but it would be a further twelve months before Alan received any letters from home visiting his father (a widower) and the friendship had blossomed with the result that the chap's former fiancée had married his father and was now his stepmother! The Americans referred to these letters as "Dear Johns". As everyone in the camp was so close, we shared our sorrows and joys and this made our difficult lives more bearable. All the mail had been censored, with portions completely blacked out. Nevertheless, by pooling information from our letters, we managed to build up some sort of idea of life back home.

Everything became a little easier now that the commandant could be approached directly through W/O Hattrick rather than through a censorious Jap interpreter. Our work at the docks and other places in and around Hakodate carried on as usual but the guards and hanchos were now very wary about punching and kicking us. We had only to tell them that we would report their behaviour to Col Emoto and they would back off. We did not realise that this was storing up trouble for ourselves.

Col Emoto kept to his word about meeting us individually and each day four men were spared work so that he could see them, two in the morning and two in the afternoon. The day that my turn came, I was called to his office early in the afternoon. He offered me tea and biscuits, then talked about Japan and how good life had been in peace time. He even asked if I had thought of staying in Japan after the war and marrying a Japanese girl – he went to great lengths to extol the virtues of his country. This was clearly a propaganda exercise but, as I had been given time off work and he was plying me with tea, biscuits and cigarettes, I was not complaining! I was in his office for two hours. At the rate of four men each day, it took months for him to see everyone in the camp and, during that time, life was definitely better than it had been under Felix. The food however was still the same monotonous rice and soup with the odd bread cake in place of the rice.

We were still working as stevedores and one day had been stealing and eating tinned salmon again to supplement our diet. The hancho that day was a friend of Kamasawa's called Takamura who was quite friendly for a Jap. We had not experienced any problems with him but, when I came out of the ship's hold for lunch, he asked whether I had been stealing salmon. Of course I said no but I think somehow he knew as he told me I was telling lies and proceeded to give me the customary beating. When I arrived back in camp I decided that I would switch to being a camp worker.

I managed to get a job working with a chap called Bert Atkinson who worked as a joiner maintaining and repairing the huts. When we paraded in the mornings the outside workers were first in line, then the camp workers, then the sick. After working in the camp for a month or so, we were on parade one morning and, after the usual counting was finished, Takamura wandered up the ranks and got his eye on me, mixed in with the camp workers. He tried to persuade me to come out to work again, saying that he would like us to be friends, but I was having nothing to do with him as he had already showed his vicious nature – I was not going to get caught again. My time as a camp worker was mostly taken up with helping Bert in his never-ending task of hut repairs for the two extremes of temperature played havoc with these wooden buildings. As the Japs didn't provide us with nails my job was wandering around the camp with a hammer and pliers removing nails that I considered superfluous and straightening them for use elsewhere. A lot of my nails came from the wooden cladding of the guardhouse and the guards' quarters where I must have reduced the number of nails by half.

On one occasion a lorry pulled into the camp on a yasume day and four of us were chosen to go with it to collect bones from the abattoir for our soup. Joe, Jack, Ianto Evans (one of the cooks) and I climbed on board and, with Billy Bennett as our guard, we set off for the abattoir in Hakodate. When we arrived, the driver and I were left in the lorry while the others went inside to collect the bones. It was a beautiful day and, as we waited, the driver sat and smoked his cigarettes in the sunshine. The smell of heaps of old hides and bones spoilt the pleasure of the perfect summer's day. After putting the bones into sacks, the others carried them to our truck where I stacked them. We had our usual look around for anything to take and, as Billy Bennett was having a drink in the office, no one took much notice of us. Joe had found a side door that led into the abattoir and there were chunks of meat on the bench and hanging on hooks. He promptly wrapped some sacking around a large piece of meat and brought it to the truck where I buried it under the sacks of bones. We finished loading and passed through the gates of the abattoir with no trouble, returning to the camp. On the way back we decided that, as the other guards could be around when we unloaded, we would give the sacking containing the meat to Ianto who would take it into the back of the cookhouse and hide it. We had no problem unloading and the sacks of bones were stacked in the cookhouse, ready to boil for stock. The meat was chopped into pieces and dropped into the pot that was destined for that evening's soup. The meat in my soup that evening made me realise how much I missed the extras which I previously had whilst working outside the camp.

After lights out I lay awake a long time trying to decide whether to go back to work outside or whether to stay as a camp worker. I would lose the job as joiner's mate with Bert but I would be able to work with Joe and the others. Not only that, but the beatings had stopped as the guards and hanchos were still afraid of being reported to Col Emoto. I was still undecided next morning when we paraded but I stayed in my position with the camp workers. I would continue for a little longer and see what happened.

A suggestion was put to Col Emoto that, if we built a path from the camp down the hillside to the bay, it could be used by the guards and POWs on yasume days. Emoto thought this was a good idea so four of us set out to dig this zigzag path down the steep hillside. We worked the same long hours as the outside workers and soon the path started to take shape. The work was quite hard as we had to clear trees and undergrowth before we could dig out the path. After a few weeks we finally finished the path and, upon reaching the pebbled shore, our guard gave us the OK for a quick swim in the bay. We didn't need to strip off for, during the summer, we dressed only in a G-string and sandals because of the heat. We spent around 15 minutes splashing about, then it was back up the path to the camp perched high above us – quite a strenuous climb. The construction of the path was quite an achievement however it was mostly used by the guards and later, when we were no longer allowed to use it, the path fell into disrepair and collapsed.

In October 1944 a group photograph of the men in each hut was taken and we were each given a copy of the photo. When the war finished and I arrived home I found that a copy of the photo had also been sent with one of my letters.

Christmas Day came and it was a yasume day. We were surprised to receive an issue of Red Cross parcels from the stores – we had imagined that the guards would have cleared these for their own use. The issue worked out at one parcel between eight men so we received one parcel for our room. Bert and I decided to make a Christmas Pudding with some of the ingredients. We used rice, chocolate, butter, dried milk and sugar. Some of the rice was ground to make flour and this, mixed with the other ingredients, was put in an army dixie tin. With its lid on, we pushed it into the bottom of the stove, among the ashes. After an hour we pulled it out and divided the contents between us. Eaten with our bowl of rice accompanied by some corned beef, and washed down with a pot of tea, served with milk and sugar, this was one of our best meals.

In the afternoon there was another surprise for WO Hattrick was called down to the admin office and came back with a sack of mail from home. This was sorted and I received three letters from my parents. It was wonderful to read the family news and know that everything was alright at home.

Several group photographs were taken at Hakodate POW Camp on 29th October 1944. Photos of five different groups of prisoners have come to light, all taken at the same location within the camp. In the background is the camp's perimeter fence and the "store room" building (with sentry box on its roof).

BACK ROW:
Nutten (RN), Carr (RAF), Turner (Army), Agro (US Navy), Grant (RAF), Purser (RAF), Bellis (Army), Welch (RAF), Self (Army)
4th ROW:
Gargano (US Navy), Anderson (US Navy), Burton (Army), McConnell (MN), Stidolph (MN), Grimshaw (Army), Stockley (Army), George (Aus), Roseveare (RAF), Glassbrook (RAF), Thomas (RAF), Robinson (RAF), Ireton (Army), McCann (Army), Flint (Army)
3rd ROW:
Mathieson (Army), Halliwell (RAF), Kenner (US Army), Burtonwood (Army), Carter (RAF), Biagini (US Navy), Hartman (US Navy), Webb (RAF), Livie (MN), Newlands (RNZAF), Henderson (RAF), Folley (RAF), Taylor (Army), Mountford (RAF), Howlett (RAF), Crane (Army), Whiteside (Army), Roe (Army), Goodwin (RAF)
2nd ROW:
Anthony (Army), Roper (Army), Hall (RAF), Cheeseman (Army), Oats (Army), Langford (Aus), Jones (RN), Derby (Army), Wright (Army), Snow (RAF), St Ledger (Army), Saint (RAF), Gorman (US MN), Gilfillan (Army), Snow (RAF)
FRONT ROW:
Motley (RN), Becker (US MN), Perkins (RAF), Tombs (RAF), Mallen (Army), Daniels (RAF), Winstanley (Army), Bray (RAF), West (MN), Melville (RAF), Teague (RAF), Greenwood (RAF), Simpson (Army), Atkinson (RAF), Street (RAF), Batt (Army), Bagley (Army), Swainson (RAF)

CHAPTER SEVENTEEN

ANOTHER CHANGE OF COMMANDANT

One night when I was doing the fire watch, Billy Bennett came into the hut. Having reported to him the number of men in the hut and that all was well, he sat down and gave me a cigarette. As we sat around the stove, he said he had heard that Col Emoto was to be moved from the camp. Next morning the whole camp was paraded and Col Emoto himself informed us that he was indeed leaving the camp. He said he had enjoyed his stay and that he hoped he would meet us again soon after the war ended. It was reported that the complaints from local civilians had reached the ears of the kempeitai and they had decided to take action.

He left the camp that evening and we were without a commandant for the next four days during which time the guards would beat us for the least mistake we made. Our new commandant duly arrived and he was an arrogant little man who spoke no English but instead harangued us in Japanese. We realised that once again life was going to become more difficult under his rule.

In recent weeks there had been quite a few air raid warnings and we could see the planes flying very high over the camp. These were all daylight raids but we were never bombed during our time in Hakodate. Americans in our camp said these planes were B-29 bombers but we had no idea where they were headed.

One night in our room after lights out, we were discussing the air raids and did not hear the duty guard approaching. It was Four Eyes and he screamed at us to get up and parade in the corridor. He went up and down the line asking what we had been talking about, prodding us with the butt of his rifle. Of course no one would even admit to talking and this drove him into a frenzy. He marched all eight of us down to the guardhouse where he explained to the sergeant that we had been talking after lights out. We stood to attention outside the guardhouse and the guards took it in turns to walk down the line punching and kicking us because no one would admit to talking. They even brought out a metal shovel they used for the stove and beat each of us around the head with it. Still no one would give in. Finally they gave up and the eight of us were marched back to our hut bruised and battered but satisfied that, even in the face of such savage questioning, we had not given in. We had marked up another score against our captors. To the Japanese, losing face is one of the worst things that can happen and that night we had certainly made Four Eyes and his colleagues lose face. At times like this we realised how much we missed Col Emoto – none of this could have happened under his command.

Our rice rations had been cut and we now had to make do with a type of red coloured millet. This was worse than the rice and the sick men could not digest it, leading to more problems with starvation and malnutrition.

One day three of us were set to work cleaning out the Japanese air raid shelter. There were empty boxes and junk to clear out but, there in the corner, was a crate of eggs. We had often seen the guards collecting boiled eggs from their cookhouse and this was clearly where they stored them to keep cool. We broke open the shells and let the raw contents slide down our throats, clearing about 6 eggs each, being careful to reduce the crate by one full layer in the hope that the cook would not notice that any eggs were missing.

It seemed as though the war would never end. Some of the chaps were reporting sick without really knowing what was wrong with them. It was depression and they had lost the will to fight any longer against the hardships we were having to bear. During this time Billy Bennett was a tonic to those of us who used to chat to him. As the American forces drew ever closer to Japan, Billy could see the writing on the wall – he was no fool. We had many a laugh at his strange suggestions of American submarines landing soldiers on the beach below the camp and spiriting all POWs away. He hoped he would also be taken, not as a prisoner but as a friend. Of course we indulged his fantasies as he was in a position to get us sugar, tea and cigarettes. We hoped he could also use his influence to stop the other guards from beating us.

A few weeks later the whole camp was summoned to parade. The commandant appeared with all the officers and the interpreter. We knew something was afoot but were not prepared for the momentous announcement that was to come. The commandant brought news that we were to move to another camp, that all outside working was cancelled, and we must prepare for the move. We had to strip out some of the cookhouse including our oven and some of the boilers. By the end of the week everything was ready and loaded on to trucks which left ahead of us. Eventually our transport arrived and we climbed aboard these army trucks. In a way it was sad to be leaving a camp that had been our home for more than two years. Also we did not know where we were going, or what type of work awaited us.

函館捕虜収容所跡

The road on the left marks the northernmost limit of the former TB isolation hospital, which became part of the POW camp in December 1942. During the war, this part of the site also served as a temporary isolation compound for typhus sufferers. The main POW camp occupied a separate and much larger parcel of land to the south – the site of the main camp can be seen in photos on pages 70 & 76.

The building on the left no longer exists. The building on the right (partly hidden by the trees) is the only structure still standing – see 2011 photo on next page.

Photo from a Hakodate local history journal, probably taken in 1980s/1990s

The one remaining building from the former Prisoner-of-War camp. Originally a quarantine office dating back to 1885, and subsequently incorporated into an isolation hospital on the same site (for cholera, and later typhus patients), it had become part of the POW camp in December 1942. Having been disused for many years, this building was renovated in 2006 to become a café with good views over the bay.

Plaque on pillar at entrance:
DAIMACHI FACILITIES
HAKODATE QUARANTINE STATION

Photos: City of Hakodate 2011

函館検疫所台町措置場（旧函館消毒所）跡

하코다테 검역소 다이마치 조처장 (구 하코다테 소독소) 터

明治18年（1885年）、内務省は防疫体制の強化を図るため、当時の主要6港（函館、横浜、神戸、下関、長崎、新潟）に日本で最初の常設消毒所を建設しました。函館では現在地に施設が建てられ、唯一残ったこの建物は事務所として使用されたものです。

明治29年（1896年）3月、函館検疫所と改称され業務をおこなってきましたが、特に昭和20年（1945年）には、敗戦により樺太方面などからの引揚者の検疫にあたり、医療や援護にとに活躍しました。

昭和43年（1968年）、検疫所は市内湾岸に落成した港湾合同庁舎内に移転し、平成4年にこの施設も廃止されました。

施設の中で唯一残ったこの事務所は、全国的にも数少ない初期港湾施設の遺構として、平成元年に市の景観形成指定建築物となっています。

函館市

THE HAKODATE QUARANTINE OFFICE IN DAI-MACHI (FORMER HAKODATE DISINFECTIONS OFFICE)

In order to strengthen the epidemic preventative measures, in 1885, the Interior Ministry established disinfections facilities in the following major trading ports: Hakodate, Niigata, Yokohama, Kobe, Shimonoseki and Nagasaki. This is where the facility was built in Hakodate. The only remaining building on the site was used as its main office.

It was renamed as the Hakodate Quarantine Office in March of 1896. Especially during the period following the end of the Second World War in 1945, it played an important role in the medical treatment and support of repatriates to Japan from Sakhalin.

The Hakodate Quarantine Office was annexed to the Joint Government Port Building in Kaigan-cho in 1968, and the facility here was demised altogether in 1992.

The building was designated as a historical building by the City of Hakodate in 1989 and represents as one of the few remnants of early port facility architecture in Japan.

CITY OF HAKODATE

Information board at roadside. Japanese "selective amnesia" has resulted in no mention being made of the POW camp that was on this site from 1942 to 1945.

CHAPTER EIGHTEEN

A NEW CAMP: Spring 1945

The journey was a long and tedious one. From what we could see out of the back of the canvas-covered truck, we were heading into the rural interior of the island. We arrived at our new camp in the evening and, after the usual hassle of tenko, we were allowed to bed down for the night in two long wooden huts. This camp was near Bibai, a long way north of Hakodate (about 200 miles by road).

Next day we were assembled and informed that we would be building additional huts to live in. The guards and a few Japanese workmen showed us how to build large frameworks on the ground and use manpower to raise these to form the sides and ends of the new hut. These were nailed together so that we had a structure resembling a box without a lid. We then had to lay beams across to strengthen the structure. The roof joists were then put in place and planks were added to support the wooden shingles that covered the roof. The shingles were nailed in place, starting with the bottom row working upwards with each row overlapping the previous one. When we arrived at the ridge, we overlapped this with a slightly larger tile, nailing it down on both sides of the ridge. We now had a wooden building about 40 feet long and 20 feet wide. Windows and doors had been made by the Jap workmen, who had been quite impressed with our efforts. They showed us how to fit the windows and doors. We had quite enjoyed this work but there was still no floor so we had to make do once again with the temporary accommodation.

For the next three or four days we continued to construct new buildings, some of which would be our living quarters and some would be for the Japs. These included a guardhouse just inside the large wooden double gates. Like Hakodate, this camp was on the side of a hill and was surrounded by a high, close-boarded wooden fence. Wood was very plentiful on Hokkaido.

Despite the continuing bad weather, our first hut was soon ready for occupation. This was a huge relief as conditions in the temporary accommodation had been very cramped. We put in sleeping platforms, one down either side of the long hut, leaving a central aisle about 4 feet in width. The wide platforms were raised up about 2 feet above the floor to eliminate draughts and dirt. The platforms were covered with close-fitting straw mats and everyone had to take boots off before stepping up there.

After about three weeks of working in the camp, all fit men were called out on parade and marched off through the small town of Bibai, eventually arriving at a coal mine – this was to be our place of work. It was a drift mine cut into the side of a hill and the coalface was reached on a train hauled by a small electric engine. Each truck was divided into compartments with wooden bench seating for six men. Before boarding the train we were each provided with a white safety helmet and a head light which clipped on to the front of the helmet, powered by a flat battery inside a case which attached to a belt fastened around the waist. There were no switches on either head light or battery so the light was constantly on. It was a big party that was going into the mine – about 100 of us boarded that train. We settled ourselves on the hard wooden benches and were whisked off at an incredible speed down the dark tunnel. The engine drew power from high voltage wires set into the roof of the tunnel and every so often the pick-up arm would hit a junction in the wire and give off a shower of sparks. Now, coming from the north east of England with its coal mining tradition, I had often heard of explosions in mines caused by a spark setting fire to coal gas and dust. Seeing the number of sparks in this confined space, I was petrified.

The train journey took about 15 minutes. When it stopped, we were ordered to get out and stand at the side of the track whilst the train disappeared back into the tunnel. We had to walk the rest of the way, down the centre of the track and, as the tunnel had been cut to accommodate small trains and small Japs, we had to beware that our metal helmets did not touch the overhead electric wires. This meant that taller men had to walk with bent knees and stooped head. The tunnel was in total darkness, lit only by the beams from our head lights. The roof was supported by wooden beams supported on pit props and these creaked and groaned under the weight they were holding up. After wending our way almost to the end of the tunnel, we came upon a network of smaller tunnels and the party was split into groups of 10 men in the charge of a Jap hancho.

My work party made its way to the coalface, about 100 yards from the main tunnel. Several Japs were digging away at the wall with picks whilst others were shovelling the coal into bogies that ran on rails down the centre of the tunnel. We were split into three groups – four men digging, four shovelling, and the other two pushing the fully-laden bogies to the main tunnel where the coal was tipped in a pile, to await loading by another gang on to wagons that were hauled to the surface by the electric engine. The work was very hard and demanding, and there was nowhere we could disappear for a rest.

The Japs kept us working without a break until lunchtime when we ate the ration of rice we had collected at the camp early that morning. Lunch was taken at the coalface and we just had to sit down on the coal to eat our food, without even a drop of water to wash our filthy hands. The only consolation was that the weather outside had been very bad, whilst here in the mine it was quite warm (but unfortunately wet). After 30 minutes we were back to the slog of digging and shovelling. In the afternoon we hit a ridge of very hard coal which considerably slowed down the digging. The Jap miners stepped in and places sticks of dynamite in holes they dug into this obstacle. Having filled in the holes around the dynamite with mud and dust, the fuses were lit and we retired to a safe distance and hid behind a bogie. There was an almighty bang and it looked as though the tunnel had collapsed but, when the dust cleared, we could see that the hard ridge had been blown out, producing loads of coal, ready to be shovelled into the bogie and moved away. We all set to work moving the coal, then it was back to the hard grind of digging once again.

This work was very different to the jobs we had in Hakodate, where you could at least claim to be "going benjo", then wander around to see if there was any food that could be stolen. Here, if you wanted the toilet, then you went somewhere in the dark tunnel – making sure it was not where you may need to sit down for lunch! And of course there was the food problem, i.e. nothing at all to steal. The work was dirty, monotonous and dangerous. In the cramped low seams I started to have attacks of claustrophobia. I decided that, if possible, I would again become a camp worker.

When we finally finished for the day, we piled our picks and shovels ready for the next day and trooped out to catch the train to the surface.

It was now dark and we had to march back to camp on the dirt roads that were full of potholes which could not be seen in the dark. When we arrived back at the camp we were of course covered in coal dust and grime but, unlike Hakodate, the Bibai camp did not have a bathhouse. So we had to fetch buckets of cold water and swill ourselves down before the evening meal was sent out by the cookhouse. This was the usual buckets of rice and thin, watery daikon soup. At least it was warm. The huts we had built were very cold and, although we had fitted three stoves in the centre aisle of each hut, they heated only the area immediately around the stove – the men with bed spaces nearby were quite warm whilst the rest were without heat. We were exhausted after our day's work so, after tenko, most of us turned in and were asleep in no time at all.

By sending all the fit men to the coal mine, only the sick were left in camp. When the Japs tried to organise work in the camp such as fetching and carrying stores, cutting wood for the cookhouse and general maintenance, they had only chronically sick people available. After tenko at 6am, breakfast at 6.30am and our usual exercise routine of 30 minutes on the square in front of the Jap quarters, we were called out on parade for work. With the others I had collected my bento box and was ready to go to the mine when WO Hattrick (we called him Chiefy) was called out by the Jap admin officer and informed that we had to provide a number of men for camp work. The result was that all the men who had been camp workers at Hakodate were told to move to the end of the parade. Bert and I were part of that group so, without even asking, I had been granted my wish and would not have to work in the coal mine.

Bert and I were detailed to maintain and repair our wooden living quarters. The Japs provided basic tools such as hammers, saws, pliers and plane but they did not seem to realise we needed nails, screws, chisels and screwdrivers. Eventually we managed to scrounge two wood chisels and some nails. We had to repair a lot of the new huts, especially the roof shingles for, although much enthusiasm had been put into building the huts, inexperience was now showing and the roofs were leaking. Another problem was the wooden wall cladding which in places was not properly overlapped, allowing the wind, rain and snow to blow through.

Work in the coal mine continued and there were two shifts working there day and night. Our rice rations had now been reduced to about half the amount the outside workers were getting and the sick were not issued with any at all. However, when the rice was sent up from the cookhouse and arrived in two buckets (one for outside workers, the other for camp workers), we divided it out equally amongst all the men so that no one did without. The outside workers were given a little more than everyone else as their jobs were very demanding. Having night shift workers needing to sleep during the day was a challenge as we could not go around repairing their huts whilst they were trying to sleep – we solved this by arranging for them to sleep in the day workers' huts whilst we did any necessary work on their own huts.

Life progressed in this fairly orderly fashion with just the odd hiccup. On one occasion six of us were working on the pitched roof of one of the huts which was next to the perimeter fence. The weather had become warmer causing some ice on the upper part of the roof to melt. Unfortunately the melt-water was blocked by ice lower down, causing it to back up and seep under the wooden shingles, pouring into the hut and wetting the sleeping mats. We had pointed boathooks and were chipping away at the ice on the lower part of the roof in an effort to allow the trapped water to escape. I was moving gingerly from one part of the roof, across to another part, when I slipped and shot down the slope with the boathook in my hand. The others thought this was a great joke until I slid completely off the roof and over the perimeter fence. I tried to climb back in but found this impossible. The only way back was through the main gates which were always kept closed and guarded. I trudged around the perimeter fence and came to the large double gates, hammering on these until they were opened by one of the Jap guards. He looked at me standing there with the boathook and seemed not to realise I was a prisoner from within his camp. He told me that I could not come in and the gate was closed in my face. I was left standing there, wondering what to do. Escaping would not be a good idea for a westerner in the middle of a Japanese island as I would stand out like a sore thumb so I banged on the gate again. The same guard opened the gate again and gestured that I should bugger off – clearly he was in no mood to be crossed and he lifted his rifle in a threatening manner. I stood my ground, kicking up a bit of a fuss, and the guard commander (a sergeant) arrived and asked what was going on. In my broken Japanese, together with much miming, I tried to explain what had happened and eventually the penny dropped. I was amazed this took so long – even if they didn't recognise me, it should have been obvious that something was not right. Anyway they hauled me in and I received a good beating. That was the end of my roofing work.

戦後まもなく。捕虜収容所を使用した仮校舎7丁目の上にありました。焼失しています。

After the war ended, the POW huts at Bibai were used for a time by the local junior high school.
Photo from a Hokkaido local history journal, taken in 1947

Wagons full of coal emerging from tunnel at the Mitsui coal mine where the Bibai POWs were sent to work.
Photo from a Hokkaido local history journal, taken in 1950s

CHAPTER NINETEEN

DESPERATION AND ESCAPE

Work in the coal mine went on day and night. Occasionally one shift had to dig the other out as there were regular cave-ins and blockages. Thank God I wasn't down there – I would have gone mad with the claustrophobic conditions if I had been trapped like that. The work was now taking its toll of the so-called fit men and we were finding that everyone was suffering from malnutrition, partly due to the lack of any contraband to supplement our camp food, but also because supplies coming into Hokkaido were being disrupted by the Allied war effort. Morale in the camp was now at it lowest ebb as we could see that the hard work and lack of food were going to finish us off. The only news we were receiving was from the Japs who kept telling us that we would never see England ever again, that we would work as slaves in Japan until we died. In our state of health we reckoned that would not take long. However the human mind and body seem to draw strength even when the odds are against survival. The long winter was at least drawing to a close and this allowed us to begin cleaning our billets and washing and drying our clothes.

The summer months brought warm and sunny weather, lifting our spirits. The discipline was still strict and rations were again cut, meaning that each worker received about half a cup of loosely packed rice. How we longed to be back in Hakodate with its fishing fleets. The only consolation was that the American bombing and blockades were having an effect on the Japs. Camp workers were having to take the places of mine workers who had become ill and I was once again in the mine, on my knees digging coal in the low and narrow seam. God, how we all hated that mine.

Discussing the future with Chiefy Hattrick, and what would happen when the war ended, he was in favour of escaping and trying to hide in the forests surrounding the camp until the Americans arrived. This was because he was convinced that the Japs would wipe out all the prisoners in the camps rather than have us testify against them for their brutality. I preferred not to believe him but, as he was the only one of our men who had access to the Jap officers, he probably had knowledge of things that could affect all of us.

During the summer, together with an American, WO Hattrick did make an escape from the camp. I remember tenko the next morning when the Japs counted us and found two men missing. They dashed around with their bead boards and kept us on the parade ground for hours until finally it sunk in that there were indeed two missing. They were most upset when they discovered that the man they trusted most had escaped – in their eyes, this loss of face was terrible. It led to a series of tenko calls where we were kept until the Japs were completely satisfied that no one else was missing.

Every day that passed without capture or any word of our escapees was a bonus to us and a slap in the face to our captors. We became convinced that the two escapees must have found a safe refuge. However after three or four days the bell clanged, calling us to a further roll call. After being counted, the camp commandant gave a long speech which was translated by the interpreter, saying that he was most offended by the escape of the two prisoners, one an officer who had been highly trusted. He said that we had been fairly treated but that in future we would not have such an easy time. We ourselves could not imagine how things could get any worse than they were already. Then, from the admin building, came guards holding two ropes attached to our friends who had escaped. The ropes were fastened to their arms which were pulled up behind their backs and connected to a noose around the neck. If their arms dropped, the noose tightened around their throats, choking them. They had been beaten and were in a terrible state, their faces covered in blood and with mud and grime on their clothes, indicating that they had been living in very rough conditions. They were shepherded around the parade ground, exhibiting them as a warning to all of us present that escape was futile. They were then taken to the guardhouse to await the arrival of the kempeitai who later took them away to their headquarters for interrogation. As all POWs had been forced to sign a document waiving our right to escape (under pain of death), we were resigned to the likelihood that our two men would be executed by the kempeitai.

CHAPTER TWENTY

THE WAR IS OVER

One day in mid August I was returning to my hut after going to the cookhouse for hot water to wash my clothes. Passing the Japanese admin building, I could see the Jap officers crowding around the radio and bowing to it. It was the first time I had seen anything like this and, returning to the billet, I remarked on it and said there must be some sort of flap going on. Later, after doing my washing, I was returning the bucket when one of the "gunsos" called me over. Expecting the customary clip around the ear for being at the cookhouse, I approached him but stopped just short of arm's reach. He told me that there would not be any workers going out that night to the coal mine and that I should pass the information to the other workers and to the cookhouse. I could not understand why but, having told the cooks, I then went back to the hut and told the other night shift workers. Of course nobody believed me and they were all waiting for the guards to come and call us for work. That call never came and the earlier day shift workers (who normally passed us on their way back) arrived in camp and asked what was going on. The guards fobbed us off, simply saying that the mine had been closed for safety reasons. We knew this must be a lie as safety had never been a concern, only maximum production of coal.

We enjoyed the unexpected yasume day and noticed that the guards were not patrolling the huts so often, mostly staying in the guardhouse and admin offices. Since Chiefy Hattrick's escape and subsequent recapture, we had no direct contact with the Jap officers. So we had no real idea what was happening. Some days later, Bert and I were called to the office and told to prepare four large signs to place around the camp. We were given a roll of black cloth and told to make framed signs about 4 feet by 6 feet, and to paint the cloth with the large yellow letters PW. We did this and were taken outside the camp with two guards and told to place the signs flat on the ground, one on each of the four sides of the camp, a short distance from the perimeter fence. We asked why we were doing this and were told it was stop American planes bombing the camp. I think this was around 24th August.

Rumours abounded that the war was over and that perhaps the Americans had landed. A few days later I got up during the night to go to the toilet but, looking for the usual guard to report where I was going, there was no guard to be found. Coming back from the toilets, I noticed that some men were gathered on the parade ground, around a huge bonfire. As they looked like our men, I went over to see what was going on and was informed that the Japs had gone. This took a while to absorb but I wandered up to guardhouse and it was completely deserted. The Japs had indeed left, and they had obviously been in a hurry – there were articles of kit strewn around the floors. After spending some time at the bonfire, chatting and smoking with the others, I discovered that one of our chaps had seen the Jap officers and guards carrying out the files and papers from the admin buildings and setting fire to them. After making certain they were burning well, they had boarded lorries and abandoned the camp. I think it was 27th August.

I returned to my hut and woke up my friends to tell them the news. We switched on the lights and talked for the rest of the night – we could celebrate as we now knew for certain the war must be over. How we had waited for this day! All the things we had planned to do to our Jap guards were forgotten in the sheer ecstasy of being able simply to sit around and talk. Dawn was breaking before I turned in and tried to sleep but it was impossible to drop off as the hut was alive with the noise of people coming and going. The cooks started early to prepare breakfast and this consisted of good portions of rice and, for once, a palatable soup.

Taking stock of our remaining supplies, we found that we had only enough rice for three or four days so scavenging parties were organised to go off looking for food. Bert and I set off from camp and explored the nearby countryside but the civilians in these areas were in a worse state than we were, and they were not at all friendly. Some of the foraging parties had better luck and turned up with chickens whereas our contribution had been just a few eggs. We had one experience where three Japs followed us for some time and their attitude was most aggressive. After we slowed the pace and ignored them, they eventually thought better of attacking us and pushed off – we were relieved as neither of us had even a stick to defend ourselves. We never went out of the camp after that unless we carried a baton for protection

– these were provided to anyone leaving the camp. We also organised our own rota of men to guard the main gates.

A couple of days later, some trucks rolled up at the camp, loaded with rice and vegetables, a present from Colonel Emoto, the former commandant at Hakodate who knew we had been transferred to Bibai and had decided to send this food from his army barracks, a gesture that was very well received. The cookhouse that evening worked overtime to give us a wonderful soup full of vegetables, to accompany our rice.

Three days had now passed since the Japs had left and, although we had seen American aircraft flying overhead, they appeared not to have seen our camp. After much discussion we agreed that we should have a barrel of petrol ready on the parade ground and, when the next plane flew overhead, we would ignite the petrol to gain their attention. So, when a plane was spotted we dropped a match into the barrel, the petrol igniting with a terrific whoosh, singeing some of our eyebrows and hair. As the plane circled, we waved and jumped about – this clearly worked as the plane proceeded to drop a small package on a tiny parachute the size of a large handkerchief. We waved and hurried over to where this had landed. It was just a box of chewing gum but, more importantly, the package included a note promising to return later.

Lunch was a rushed affair as everyone wanted to be outside, ready for the return of the American plane. We had to wait until mid afternoon and this time there were three planes. The first dropped a weighted pouch that had a trailing red ribbon, the pouch containing a folded sheet addressed to the "senior prisoner of war". This confirmed that the plane's crew were from Squadron VC-99 based at Ominato (we had no idea where this was but I now know it is near the northern end of Honshu, Japan's main island) and that they were going to drop supplies as long as we needed them. Large canisters had also been dropped but, as soon as the parachutes opened, the harnesses broke and the canisters dropped like bombs so we had to scatter to avoid injury! We collected all the canisters and, even though some things had been damaged, most of the contents were in good shape. There were tins of fruit, fish, meat, soup and vegetables, also chocolate, jam, marmalade, coffee, dried milk, butter, cheese, dried egg powder and K-rations. Medicines, vitamin tablets, soap, cigarettes and clothing were also dropped. Attached to a smaller parachute was a box that contained a walkie-talkie with instructions on its use – it was pre-set so that we could talk to the aircraft overhead – this was our first contact with the outside world.

The Americans had thought of everything, even DDT powder – we had some sport when we dusted this over our blankets and watched the fleas jumping then dying. They had made our lives a misery and we were now returning the compliment. There was real excitement that evening with the food that came from the cookhouse (the cooks really excelled themselves) – it was our first taste of western food for some time. We sat all night drinking chocolate laced with spoonfuls of sugar, chain-smoking the cigarettes, and talking about the contact we now had with the Americans. We could now look forward to getting back home to our loved ones. There had however been one or two mishaps in the food drop. One chap who was lying in the hospital hut had his leg broken when a crate of chocolate plunged through the roof of the hut. Other huts had also been damaged but fortunately there was only the one casualty.

Next morning around 7am we heard planes overhead. We heard on the walkie-talkie that we should clear the parade ground and keep clear until the last aircraft had dropped its load. The first plane then swooped low over the camp and released the spare fuel holders attached to its wings. The other planes followed then, swooping again over the camp, the leader told us they would deliver to our camp every morning – with compliments of the forces on his aircraft carrier. After the planes had gone, we broke open the containers and found them stacked solid with freshly-baked bread. This was a very pleasant addition to our food stocks so, for breakfast, we had fruit juice, fried spam with scrambled eggs, followed by bread and butter with marmalade, all washed down with hot sweet coffee. I will always remember that meal as it was the first good breakfast in 3½ years. The Americans were certainly looking after us.

The American air drops continued for a few days then, around 14th September, we were requested to make our way to the airfield at Sapporo where aircraft would be waiting to fly us out of Hokkaido. We gathered our few possessions and next day we marched out, heading for the railway station in Bibai. The official at the station was a typically unhelpful Jap – in any kind of uniform they were used to being little dictators. His message was that there was no train to take us to Sapporo that day, perhaps there would be one tomorrow. After some "persuasion" he revealed that a local train was due in five minutes and, when it arrived, all passengers were told to alight. We then commandeered the train and, with two of our men in the cab of the engine to keep the Japanese driver and fireman working, we set off for a two hour run to Sapporo. We arrived around lunchtime and the American air force had trucks standing by, all ready to take us out to the airfield. Once there, we found that lunch had been prepared for us and we tucked into a superb meal of soup followed by chicken, potatoes, peas and carrots with ice cream as a dessert. After lunch we had to wait for the aircraft to arrive as they had been held up on their way north.

This is the weighted pouch and folded message from US task force commander, Admiral Harold Montgomery Martin. With its bright red trailing ribbon, it was dropped by US Air Force Squadron VC-99. Alan was successful in retrieving it and always treasured this memento of his eventual liberation from life as a POW.

TO: SENIOR PRISONER OF WAR

WE ARE GOING TO DROP YOU SUPPLIES AS LONG AS YOU NEED THEM. THE WAR IS OVER - JAPAN HAS SURRENDERED UNCONDITIONALLY AND AMERICAN TROOPS ARE OCCUPYING WHOLE COUNTRY. HELP SHOULD BE ARRIVING AT YOUR CAMP VERY SHORTLY. PRESENT NEAREST AMERICAN FORCES AT OMINATO. FIRST ORDER TO JAPANESE WAS POW WELFARE AND THEY ARE SUPPOSED TO TURN CAMP OVER TO YOU AND TRANSPORT YOU TO NEAREST PORT FOR EMBARKATION. WE'VE A LARGE CARRIER TASK FORCE COVERING OCCUPATION. ADMIRAL FLETCHER WITH MAIN BODY IS SETTING UP HEADQUARTERS IN OMINATO AND WILL SEND LAND FORCES TO YOU AS SOON AS POSSIBLE. IF YOU CAN SPELL OUT ANY URGENT REQUIREMENTS WE'LL TRY AND DELIVER. TWO WALKIE-TALKIE RADIOS HAVE BEEN DROPPED YOU SET ON FREQUENCY 3895. KEEP YOUR CHIN UP AND WE WILL DO EVERYTHING IN OUR POWER TO GET YOU OUT AND HOME AS SOON AS POSSIBLE. BE SURE TO KEEP RECORD OF ANY MISTREATMENT. WE WILL MAKE THEM PAY DEARLY. GOOD LUCK.

ADMIRAL H.M. MARTIN
COMMANDER TASK FORCE 44

Dropped by —
P.A. Seibold Pilot
Norman L. Baker AMM 2/c
W.L. Gunlock ARM 3/c
R. Jewell AMM 2/c
VC 99

Message dropped in the weighted pouch – this was the first confirmation from American forces that they knew of the existence of the Prisoner-of-War camp at Bibai. It heralded the dropping of vital supplies (and some very welcome luxuries), all of which kept the POWs going during the first half of September 1945 prior to regaining their freedom.

CHAPTER TWENTY ONE

RETURNING HOME

The Americans used the time to begin the task of debriefing, wanting information on any serious mistreatment that could be used as evidence of war crimes. In our eyes, this included nearly every Japanese officer and guard we had come into contact with. One exception was Colonel Emoto and everyone from the camp put in a good word for him. When the planes arrived we were divided into groups of around 40 men and, with the minimum of baggage, we boarded these Dakota aircraft to fly down to Tokyo. The inside of the plane was very basic, presumably stripped out during the war to accommodate the maximum number of troops. The canvas seating was down both sides of the fuselage so that we all faced towards the middle, and there were no seat belts. None of this bothered us as we were only interested in getting out of Hokkaido and on our way home. The crew on this plane were pilot, co-pilot and a dog that belonged to one of them, a small terrier that sat on the lap of the co-pilot. During take-off some of us at the back of the aircraft had to move forward to lighten the tail weight, then return to our seats when we were airborne.

We roared down the runway and left the soil of Hokkaido, circling the airfield while the other planes took off. We then turned and headed south, passing over Hakodate on the way. Over the main island of Honshu the crew appeared to be lost and we put down at a small airfield. Three Japanese officers marched out to meet us and it was clear that they had not seen any Americans and thought we had arrived to take over the airfield. We asked about accommodation and food for the night but they had only rice and tinned oranges for a meal and their small guardhouse for accommodation. A decision was made not to stay but to press on to Tokyo.

At the end of the runway was a very large mountain. Our plane was the first to attempt take off and once again we tail-enders had to move forward so I was standing just behind the pilot and navigator. The engines were started and revved up with the brakes on until it seemed as if the plane would rattle itself to pieces. The brakes were then released and we shot down the very short runway towards the mountain which loomed at the end of it. Just when I was thinking we did not have enough power to lift off, I felt my legs bending at the knees as the pilot pulled the stick back and up we went. Looking out of the cockpit, I saw the mountainside and we seemed to be running up the side of it. We then banked away to the left and started climbing into the sun. Circling the airfield to watch the other planes take off we could see how difficult the manoeuvre had been.

We eventually arrived over Tokyo Bay where we flew over the battleship USS Missouri on which General MacArthur had accepted the surrender of Japanese forces on 2nd September. After landing at Tokyo airport we said our farewells to the crews of our planes and were shepherded into one of the hangars. This had been prepared as a reception area where everyone was put through a de-lousing procedure of showers and disinfectant. We were issued with two new uniforms of the US Army, together with boots and underwear. Our own clothing was taken away for decontamination. We were then invited into the mess hall for food. The Americans certainly knew how to live – there was so much food on offer that we didn't know where to start! They had roast chickens, pork, beef, potatoes and greens – as much as you could eat – followed by ice cream and gallons of coffee or coca-cola. Cigarettes were handed out in packs of 20, plus cigars.

We tried to get some sleep but this was practically impossible. After sleeping on thin mats on a hard floor for 3½ years, very few could get to sleep on a proper bed with springs. Also, every time I turned over, I thought I was going to fall out! Next morning, after a memorable breakfast of bacon and scrambled eggs with toast and marmalade, a few of us decided to wander around the airfield – we were not allowed into Tokyo as it had been badly fire-bombed. Whilst looking around the airfield, we came upon an area which was still out of bounds. We were informed that Japanese soldiers had barricaded themselves in a complex of tunnels burrowed under the airfield and the Americans could only get them out with flamethrowers. The stench of kerosene and burnt flesh was still hanging in the air and the Americans were unsure whether there may still be some Japs in the tunnels, hence the exclusion order. We also saw some Japanese flying bombs consisting of a long torpedo-like bomb with short stubby wings, a tailfin and rudder. The cockpit had a perspex hood fitted with a padlock. As far as I could gather, the pilot of these kamikaze planes was padlocked in and cast off from a mother aircraft, his role being to glide down and crash into our ships.

Some of the earlier arrivals had already left for home and we were given a choice of returning direct by aircraft carrier via India and the Suez Canal or going to the USA and then home. As I had an aunt who lived in Long Island (New York) I decided to go via the USA so that I would be able to meet her. We were supposed to fly out to Okinawa but, as it was the typhoon season, most flights were cancelled. After waiting for a week, we were moved to the docks and boarded a US Navy ship which took us to the Philippines, arriving around 26th September. We ended up in a large "prisoner of war reception camp" run by the Australians and Americans, about 15 miles outside Manila, where we were accommodated in large tents.

Reception camp in the Philippines September/October 1945
Photo: Australian War Memorial (118984)

Our stay in Manila should have been brief but again there were problems with typhoons, compounding the difficulties that were due to a shortage of available vessels. Although we were not confined to camp and could travel around anywhere, we were desperately short of money. The best we could manage was hitching a ride into the city for a few beers, then back to the camp. We all had vaccination and inoculation jabs while staying at this camp. In a letter received from England, I found there had been two recent marriages, one being my sister Patsy and the other my cousin Don. I used the time in Manila to write letters to my parents and sisters, including a telegram that would be routed via Melbourne Australia!

The typhoons continued to blow, with ferocious winds and torrential rain buffeting the tents at our camp. On 6th October, Lady Mountbatten came to visit the camp and she met and talked to all the British former-POWs. We were still waiting for transport to arrive. A British aircraft carrier departed for Canada with a large contingent but I was not on the list. I was becoming rather impatient waiting for something to happen but at last I was included in a new draft for transport to San Francisco. After nearly two weeks of lazing around and eating good food, I had started to put on weight and, like most of the men, was now looking more presentable. We packed our kit and next day were bussed out to the docks.

Our transport to the USA was the USS Marine Shark, a "liberty ship" fitted out as a troop carrier and coming into the Philippines on her maiden voyage. We boarded at dusk on (I think) 9th October, sailing the following day with approximately 3000 people on board – there were around 1500 British, 1300 Americans and 200 women, some of them former internees. The holds were full of collapsible beds and nothing else. In the dining halls, food was served cafeteria-style direct on to metal trays with separate food compartments. By mid October, thanks to proper food, I was up to 11 stones in weight, having gained around 3 stones in less than two months.

USS Marine Shark

The ship called in at Honolulu where repairs were carried out to the propeller shaft which had developed a fault. These repairs were started immediately after berthing and completed in less than two days, leaving us no time to see the island. Once again we sailed at dusk, passing the famous Diamond Head on our way out to the ocean. The gremlins had not finished with us for, during the night, an engineer fell asleep on duty and a boiler blew out. We were now reduced to just half speed. Work started to repair the damage but the ship wallowed in the sea as a typhoon started to brew up. The hatches were battened down but we still had to queue up on deck for our food, not a pleasant experience in such bad weather. To make matters worse, oil from the gun wells (the guns had been removed) started to leak over the decks. Our US army boots, with their rubber soles and heels, were treacherous on this very slippery surface. As the typhoon intensified, the ship rolled precariously and at times the deck rails seemed to dip under the waves which lashed across the deck. The storm continued for three days with everyone in our hold being seasick. Food was of little consequence which in a way was just as well because the stores of both food and water were now running low. The drinking water was stored in ballast tanks and as we drained the tank so the ship rose higher in the sea and lost much of its stability.

When the typhoon finally passed and the sun came out, things got back to normal – apart from the slow progress we were making across the Pacific. We had on board a number of former POWs who had been crew members on HMS Prince of Wales and HMS Repulse, both of which had been sunk by the Japs in 1941. One of the officers offered to try and sort out the problems in the engine room on condition that his men would be allowed to operate independently. This was agreed by the American captain and our men set to work. After two days and nights they had succeeded in patching up the damaged boiler and the ship started to make headway at about two-thirds of normal speed.

Food was becoming a problem and the cooks had to resort to serving us mainly rice or potatoes. There was almost a mutiny when we found we would have to eat rice once again! However the sun was shining, the sea was calm, and we were making good progress – all grumbles soon died away. After what seemed like an endless voyage we eventually saw land and the excitement grew, not only for those of us seeing

America for the first time but also amongst the American servicemen who were almost home after much bitter fighting.

We had been informed on the ship's intercom that we would be arriving in San Francisco the next day and couldn't contain our delight as we drew ever nearer. Next morning we sailed under the Golden Gate Bridge and into the bay with small boats joining us. On the walls of the grim-faced prison at Alcatraz were "Welcome Home" banners. We arrived at Angel Island where the Americans had set up a large transit camp with all the facilities required to accommodate returning service personnel. We were shown our sleeping quarters and the dining hall. The food was everything we had dreamed about during our time in captivity. There were whole chickens, together with all the trimmings, for every man. This was followed by peaches and ice cream, coffee and doughnuts. Second helpings were available for anyone wanting them. It was our first meal in the USA and nothing was spared to make sure every man was fed to his satisfaction. Cigarettes and cigars were also provided and, when we retired for the night, we were full of praise for our American hosts. On 2nd November I managed to send my family a telegram telling them I had arrived safely.

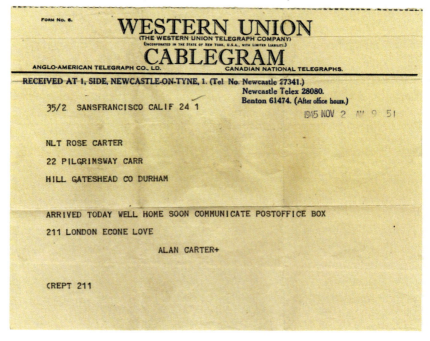

From San Francisco we were sent by train to Tacoma, near Seattle, and spent about four days there. Once again the accommodation and food were first class. The problem was that we were short of cash as a result of the British Government's policy of keeping money in Britain. However, by selling souvenirs such as swords and daggers that we intended to take home, some of us acquired US dollars and these paid for our nights out on the town. There were also trips to United Service clubs which laid on dances where there were free soft drinks.

After our stay at Tacoma, we resumed our train journey and travelled north into Canada, through the Rocky Mountains. We stopped for breaks of one or two hours in places such as Edmonton and Saskatoon and, after travelling for five days, crossed back into the USA to our destination of New York. The food and attention we were given on this wonderful train journey was simply fantastic – the hospitality of the Canadians will always be remembered. As will the reception we received when we boarded the Queen Mary for our voyage home. The ocean liner had been refitted during the war as a troop ship and was painted in battleship grey.

RMS Queen Mary in wartime livery – this was the final leg of the lengthy journey back to England in November 1945
Photo: Australian War Memorial (004302)

For the first time since leaving Japan, we were now under the command of the British and the change was a shock. Each of us was now just a number, rather than a person. The first intimation of this was that, instead of cafeteria-style meal service, there was a call for table waiters. As no one would volunteer for these duties we were informed over the loudspeakers that no food would be served until such volunteers came forward. I was allocated to a cabin with 15 men sharing the room, the beds being stacked in tiers – three tiers, each with five beds. Lunch time came and, as no one would be a table waiter, no meal was served – what a difference to our treatment elsewhere. When it was time for the next meal, we were allowed to collect this at the serving hatch and take it to a table. We had to take our turn in a rota of fire guards in the ship's corridors. After five days the ship docked at Southampton on 18th November.

Almost four years after leaving, I had finally arrived back in England.

BUCKINGHAM PALACE

    The Queen and I bid you a very warm welcome home.

    Through all the great trials and sufferings which you have undergone at the hands of the Japanese, you and your comrades have been constantly in our thoughts. We know from the accounts we have already received how heavy those sufferings have been. We know also that these have been endured by you with the highest courage.

    We mourn with you the deaths of so many of your gallant comrades.

    With all our hearts, we hope that your return from captivity will bring you and your families a full measure of happiness, which you may long enjoy together.

George R.I.

September 1945.

Photo believed to have been taken on way home in October/November 1945. Alan is on the left and, although there are no names on the back of the photo to help with identification, the others could be Tom Glassbrook, Joe Purser and Jack Roseveare. The location is not known so further information would be most welcome (also confirmation whether these are the US Army uniforms previously mentioned as having been issued to the former POWs).

JAPANESE WAR CRIMINALS RELEASED

Two Japanese war criminals, Yoshika Yagi (left) and Toshio Hatakeyma, walking out of Sugamo prison last week. The United States approved the release. Yagi was serving 15 years' imprisonment and Hatakeyma 12 years. They are now on parole.

Jap War Criminals To Be Paroled

TOKYO — (U.P.) — Two Japanese war criminals will be paroled within a few days, the first to be released since the end of the allied occupation, the Japanese government announced today.

The paroles were approved by the U.S.-Japanese war criminal commission set up recently by President Truman. The parolees are Toshio Hatakeyama, 63, and Yoshika Yagi, 37.

Hatakeyama, a former army colonel, served as chief of the Hakodate prisoner of war camp. He was sentenced to 12 years in 1948.

Yagi, an army civilian employe, was sentenced to 15 years in 1946.

There are still 830 war criminals still serving sentences in Sugamo prison.

Press cuttings from October/November 1952 reporting the release on parole of Toshio Hatakayama, the original camp commandant at Hakodate 1942-1944. He had been sentenced to 12 years hard labour at a war crimes trial but was released after just 6 years in prison.

County Borough of Gateshead.

WELCOME HOME COMMITTEE

Presented to ALAN CARTER.

with the thanks of the Gateshead Welcome Home Committee on behalf of the Townspeople of Gateshead as an expression of gratitude for services rendered during the War, 1939-1945.

Dated this 31st day of May 1947.

Mayor,
Chairman, Welcome Home Committee.

Town Clerk,
Honorary Secretary, Welcome Home Committee.

Alan with his dog Koura, c.1947/1948

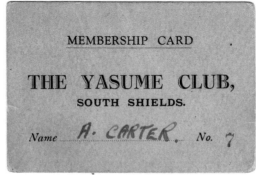

Yasume Club gave former Far East POWs an opportunity to keep in touch with one another

Alan and Teresa's wedding in 1954

Alan with son Paul c.1958/1959

Tessa and Alan in France (in 2002)

Alan in 2009

Further Information

- RMS Warwick Castle was later sunk by a German U-boat, 200 miles off Portugal, in November 1942. The troops on board had been disembarked for the North African campaign a few days earlier and the ship was returning to the Clyde.
- Batavia was the Dutch name for Jakarta, the city that is now the Indonesian capital.
- Suggested further reading on the RAF's deployment in Java and Sumatra: The London Gazette no.38216 – *"REPORT ON THE AIR OPERATIONS DURING THE CAMPAIGNS IN MALAYA AND NETHERLAND EAST INDIES FROM 8TH DECEMBER 1941 TO 12TH MARCH 1942"* which can be found at:
  www.ibiblio.org/hyperwar/UN/UK/LondonGazette
- The Tofuku Maru has sometimes been noted as Tojuku Maru.
- There were several POW camps in Hakodate: Alan was Prisoner 248 in the main camp at 27 Dai-machi (on the hill leading up to the city crematorium).
- There were 114 deaths among the POWs despatched by the Japanese from Java to Hakodate main camp. 25 died in transit on the Tofuku Maru in October/November 1942 and a further 47 died at the Kokura Military Hospital in December 1942 after becoming seriously ill on board the Tofuku Maru (the number of deaths on the Tofuku Maru may have been understated – the war crimes report mentioned a figure of 27). No fewer than 42 died during their time as prisoners at the Hakodate main camp.
- It was Spring 1943 before Alan's family were notified that he was a POW, a full year after he had been taken prisoner. Alan had to wait a further year before he received news from home.
- The camp's original commandant, nicknamed Felix, was Col. Toshio Hatakayama (his name often appears as Hatakeyama). After the war, he was tried for war crimes by the Yokohama

and Terry Willis – and to my wife Wendy for proof reading the text and for her patience and support during the transcription and preparation of this publication.

It has been quite a challenge to assemble everything and I really wish I had found time to do so while Dad was still alive. I just hope that this book does justice to the very human story of his personal battle for survival, and the comradeship he shared with his fellow POWs, during those 3½ years of captivity.

Images are credited where the photographer is known.

I would welcome further information concerning the following:

- 605 Squadron and its bases in Shropshire and Warwickshire
- Journey from Scotland via Cape Town to the Far East, December 1941 to February 1942
- Java & Sumatra: final weeks of freedom, February/March 1942
- Boei Glodok POW prison, March to October 1942
- Dai Nichi Maru "hell ship" from Java to Singapore, October 1942
- Changi POW Camp, October 1942
- Tofuku Maru "hell ship" from Singapore to Japan, October/November 1942
- Hakodate POW Camp, December 1942 to Spring 1945
- Bibai POW Camp, Spring 1945 until liberation in September 1945
- Manila reception camp, September/October 1945
- Marine Shark voyage from Manila to San Francisco, October/November 1945
- Time spent in San Francisco and Tacoma
- Train journey from Tacoma through Canada to New York, November 1945
- Homebound voyage on Queen Mary, November 1945
- Demobilisation process, November 1945 to May 1946

My contact email is: paul@pcarter.net

178

- He was mystified how the Japanese, with a reputation for being a polite and gentle race, could have treated prisoners so inhumanely. Perhaps it was a way of showing their disdain for those who had allowed themselves to be captured – their Senjinkun military code of conduct included the instruction: "Never live to experience shame as a prisoner – by dying you will avoid leaving a stain on your honour".
- He was also very cynical about the way the Japanese have never really come to terms with their past – and how their denial of what actually happened has led to succeeding generations being brought up in blissful ignorance of the horrors of the camps which were run by their forebears. He had no problem with younger Japanese people but was frustrated by how little they knew.
- He had a relaxed retirement although his later years consisted mainly of caring for Tessa, who had become increasingly frail.
- Alan died suddenly in June 2010 on his way to visit Tessa in hospital. He was a devoted husband and father and is very much missed by his family.

Full names of other POWs who are mentioned (where known):
Joe Purser, Jack Roseveare, Danny Meaghan, Ginger Edwards, Tom Glassbrook, Jimmy Wright, Bert Atkinson and Americans Harry Agro & Frank Hartman.

I would like to thank Nigel Brown (son of Daniel Brown, Hakodate/Bibai POW), Frank Planton (POW at Hakodate and later at Ohasi), Colin Stevenson (son of Harry C Stevenson, Hakodate/Bibai POW), Ronald van der Waag (son of Leo van der Waag, Hakodate/Bibai POW), Richard Whymark (grandson of Jack Snow, Hakodate/Bibai POW), Graham Wilson (webmaster of 2/30 Battalion, Australian Imperial Forces Association).

My thanks also to family members for their information and photos – special thanks must go to Molly Chalton, Pauline Potts

177

celebrated more than 6 months previously, so there was no heroes' welcome.

- Before boarding the Queen Mary, he did meet his great aunt.
- Alan's promotion from AC1 to LAC (leading aircraftman) was confirmed after his return, backdated to 15 September 1945, believed to be the day he was finally liberated from the POW camp.
- He was discharged from service on 5 May 1946 and awarded a £70 payment.
- Alan resumed work at Angus Errington in Gateshead, progressing from warehouseman to become the company's main salesman, selling paper and packaging products. With his wry sense of humour, he named his Alsatian puppy Koura (a brusque call to attention, frequently used by Alan's Japanese captors).
- A devout Catholic, in 1950 he went on a pilgrimage to Rome as a way of giving thanks for surviving the war.
- Alan joined the Yasume Club branch in South Shields, the club having been set up by former Far East POWs as a way of keeping in touch. He also joined the Civil Defence.
- Alan moved away from Gateshead in 1954 when he married the love of his life, Teresa. They bought a new bungalow in one of the outer suburbs of Newcastle and their only child Paul was born in 1956. Ellison Street in Gateshead, which had been Alan's first home, was cleared to make way for the 1960s multi-storey car park that featured in the film "Get Carter" (no relation!) – this was demolished in 2010.
- Alan's life after the war was a happy and fulfilling one, although thoughts of his time as a POW were never far away.
- He always tried to concentrate on the more humorous episodes of his time in the Far East, rather than dwell on the many horrors he experienced and observed.
- In 1985, he retired from his job as a sales manager and started to chronicle his wartime memories.
- Alan never forgave the Japanese nation for the inhumane way they treated the POWs.

military commission and sentenced to 12 years hard labour. The report of his trial can be found at: www.online.uni-marburg.de/icwc/yokohama/Yokohama%20No.%207203.pdf
Others tried and sentenced for war crimes at Hakodate main camp included Teruichi Saito (Billy Bennett), Nobuhiro Miyakawa (Yankee Clipper), Seiichi Yutani (Yah Yah), Kiyamatsu Suda (Mineral Charlie), Shooichi Sasaki, Ryuma Hirano, Sadeo Sakano. Also medics Tsutomi Shiba and Shigeru Aona.

- The second commandant was Lt/Col. Shigeo Emoto (March 1944 to April 1945). Not only was his regime more sympathetic to the plight of the POWs but he also testified against Col. Hatakayama at his trial. The third commandant was Col. Atsuro Hosoi.
- At least five groups of POWs were photographed on 29th October 1944 – this was highly unusual in the Japanese POW camps and the reason is not known. Perhaps it was for propaganda purposes, or to coincide with a Red Cross visit.
- Winters in Hokkaido are notoriously cold and 1944/1945 was Japan's worst winter in 25 years, adding to the challenges faced by the POWs.
- When the camp moved to Bibai it was sited at 1-2695 Bibai-cho, believed to be on a hillside to the east of Bibai town. Work was at the Mitsui coal mine.
- With defeat looking increasingly likely, orders had been issued by the Japanese high command during 1944-45 to kill all prisoners at short notice in the event of a landing and advance of Allied forces. Unpopular as it may be to say it in these politically correct times, the atomic bombs at Hiroshima and Nagasaki undoubtedly saved the lives of many thousands of POWs. Alan was always thankful that Japanese surrender came swiftly after the bombs had been dropped – he believed it had prevented him from being executed.
- While his reception in the USA and Canada was truly memorable, his arrival back in England was a very low key affair – the war was long over, victory in Europe having been

175